RUG HOOKING PRESENTS

preserving the past in primitive rugs

By Barbara Evans Brown

EDITION III • RUG HOOKING MAGAZINE'S FRAMEWORK SERIES

Author and Fiber Artist
Barbara Evans Brown

Editor
Patrice A. Crowley

Book Designer
Cher Williams

Photography
David Allen
Michael Brown
Chris Smith

Assistant Editor
Brenda J. Wilt

Publisher
David Detweiler

Rug Hooking
1300 Market Street, Suite 202
Lemoyne, PA 17043-1420
(717) 234-5091
(800) 233-9055
www.rughookingonline.com

Printed in China

Dedication

This book is dedicated in loving memory to my dad, Edward White Evans (January 1, 1919 - October 24, 1998). His happy memories of growing up in Boston during the 1920s led me to design and hook rugs with a new theme and to document in this book the evolution of my design and hooking efforts. This book and my rugs depicting Dad's stories have prompted my mom to recount tales of her youth that will also be recorded in wool. My parents are an inspiration to their children and grandchildren, and these rugs will keep their memories alive for generations.

Acknowledgments

I thank my Mom, Ruth Noden Evans, for instilling in me a love of needlework; my sister Carolyn for introducing me to rug hooking; Mary Paul Wright for teaching me all I needed to know about rug hooking and urging me to pursue my interests; and my husband, Michael, for providing the opportunity and encouragement to develop my rug hooking skills.

About the Publisher

Rug Hooking magazine, the publisher of *Preserving the Past in Primitive Rugs*, welcomes you to the rug hooking community. Since 1989 *Rug Hooking* has served thousands of rug hookers around the world with its instructional, illustrated articles on dyeing, designing, color planning, hooking techniques, and more. Color photographs of beautiful rugs old and new, profiles of teachers, designers, and fellow rug hookers, and announcements of workshops, exhibits, and gatherings appear in each issue of the magazine.

Rug Hooking has responded to its readers' demand for more inspiration and information by going online, publishing pattern books, revising its Sourcebook listing of teachers, guilds, and schools, initiating the Framework Series of in-depth instructional books, and continuing to produce the competition-based book series *A Celebration of Hand-Hooked Rugs. Preserving the Past in Primitive Rugs* represents but a fragment of the incredible art that is being produced today by women and men of all ages.

For more information on rug hooking and *Rug Hooking* magazine, call or write us at the address on page 1.

What Is Rug Hooking?

Some strips of wool. A simple tool. A bit of burlap. How ingenious were the women and men of ages past to see how such humble household items could make such beautiful rugs.

Although some form of traditional rug hooking has existed for centuries, this fiber craft became a fiber art only in the last 150 years. The fundamental steps have remained the same: A pattern is drawn onto a foundation, such as burlap or linen. A zigzag line of stitches is sewed along the foundation's edges to keep them from fraying as the rug is worked. The foundation is then stretched onto a frame, and strips of wool, which may have been dyed by hand, are pulled through it with an implement that resembles a crochet hook inserted into a wooden handle. The compacted loops of wool remain in place without the need for knots or stitching. The completed rug may have its edges whipstitched with cording and yarn as a finishing touch to add durability.

Despite the simplicity of the basic method, highly intricate designs can be created with it. Using a multitude of dyeing techniques to produce unusual effects, or various hooking methods to create realistic shading, or different widths of wool

Editor's Note

MANY RUG HOOKERS MET BARBARA BROWN for the first time in the September/October 1996 issue of *Rug Hooking* magazine. That issue, which featured some of her Kennebunkport rugs, was a huge hit, selling out quickly. We were captivated by her simple patterns and warm hues, and entranced by her easy, humble, storytelling approach to teaching with words and pictures.

Fortunately for us all, Barbara has written an entire book in that style, walking us through her development as a fiber artist and walking us past her beautiful primitive rugs. On our walk we learn not only how she designs and plans the colors for her rugs, but also how we can do the same for our own rugs. Whether she is showing us how to draw a building or someone else's memory of a long-ago event, Barbara patiently leads us through the process of discovery.

One of the most important perspectives she gives us is that it is OK to make mistakes. Second thoughts about a rug's pattern or colors can serve as mile markers on our journey to becoming better rug hookers. In a competitive, perfection-oriented world such as ours it is reassuring to hear that from someone so gifted. And that's really what Barbara's book is all about: Inspiration, be it from surroundings or recollections, leads to creation, then reevaluation and the continued pursuit of preserving the impermanent.

Barbara's intent is to preserve the past in her hooked rugs and to encourage others to do the same. We are glad she has preserved her rugs and her wisdom in this book.—*Patrice Crowley*

to achieve a primitive or formal style, today's rug hookers have gone beyond making strictly utilitarian floor coverings to also make wallhangings, vests, lampshades, purses, pictorials, portraits, and more. Some have incorporated other kinds of needlework into their hooked rugs to fashion unique and fascinating fiber art that's been shown in museums, exhibits, and galleries throughout the world.

The rugs seen in this book were hooked with a wide—$1/4"$ to $3/8"$—cut of wool. This style is but one of the many employed by the thousands of rug hookers worldwide. For a good look at what contemporary rug hookers are doing with yesteryear's craft—or to learn how to hook your own rug—pick up a copy of *Rug Hooking* magazine, or visit our web site at www.rughookingonline.com. (To learn more about *Rug Hooking*, see page 2.) Within the world of rug hooking—and *Rug Hooking* magazine—you'll find there's a style to suit every taste and a growing community of giving, gracious fiber artists who will welcome you to their gatherings.—*Patrice Crowley*

barbara
brown

PHOTOGRAPH BY MICHAEL BROWN.

my journey as a rug hooker

Of all the hobbies I have delved into over the years, not one has held my interest or given me as much satisfaction as rug hooking has. That's why I am excited about having the opportunity, through this book, to share with you my passion for primitive pictorial rugs.

I HAVE BEEN HOOKING PRIMI-TIVE RUGS for about 14 years. Long ago, while I was still living at home with my parents, I used to cut pictures of primitive hooked rugs out of magazines. I liked the rugs, but neither I nor any one I knew had an inkling about how they were made. It was by coincidence that, years later, my sister Carolyn began to hook rugs after purchasing supplies and a partially finished rug at a yard sale held by an elderly woman who was no longer hooking. Carolyn, wanting to finish the rug, obtained the name of a teacher who showed her the basics and familiarized her with the National Guild of Pearl K. McGown Rug Hookrafters and its teacher certification program. She finished not only that first rug but also many more after attending rug camps every summer and becoming a certified McGown teacher.

I loved Carolyn's rugs, but they were done in the tapestry hooking style. Tapestry hooking is done with very narrow (as narrow as $3/32$") strips of wool fabric, and the subjects of many of these rugs are floral and Oriental designs. At McGown rug camps my sister learned to dye wool fabric and hook it into perfectly shaded realistic flowers and leaves. Somehow I never saw the connection between what she was doing and those pictures I had torn out of magazines years earlier. By this time I had moved from my parents' house, married Michael, acquired a dog and cat, and I knew that the beautiful rugs Carolyn was hooking wouldn't last long at my house.

One day, after my husband and I had moved from Andover, Massachusetts, to Atlanta, Georgia, Carolyn came to visit, bringing with her the name of a rug hooking teacher in my area. The teacher was located on the other side of town, and we got desperately lost trying to find her home. When we did meet up with her she suggested another teacher closer to my home; she, in turn, led me to Mary Paul Wright. Mary Paul taught me everything I ever needed to know about rug hooking. Unlike the other two Atlanta teachers, who hooked in the tapestry style, Mary Paul was hooking primitive rugs, just the kind I had seen in those magazines. They were simpler and more straightforward than tapestry style rugs, in deeper, more durable colors and textures.

I didn't accomplish much that first autumn, but in early

I want to encourage you to start a journey of your own that will result in hooked heirlooms prized by future generations for the memories they evoke.

Little Andy
35" x 20"
Single-thickness, hand-cut wool strips hooked through primitive linen.

PHOTOGRAPH BY CHRIS SMITH.

MY HUSBAND HAS AN OLD RED TRUCK and I have photos of our cocker spaniel, Andy, sitting in the driver's seat of it. I had tried to draw a rug based on the photos but I got bogged down in details, such as the bumpers, lights, and so forth. Then I realized that truck details and an accurate rendition of the dog were not important. Although I am aware of the need to simplify, I still forget to ignore unimportant details at times.

The truck, which is actually bright red, was hooked in a red-and-black tweed to age and soften it. The tires were hooked in a gray plaid containing minor amounts of black, red, and oatmeal. That combination of colors produces a texture different from the red-tweed truck body and the solid black fenders. But repeating the red and black truck colors in the gray tires ties all three elements together.

When color planning a rug, look for tweeds and plaids whose major colors are different from each other, but whose minor colors are the same as other major colors in the rug. The result is usually coordinated variety. The olive-green plaid used to hook the lower background has red, gold, and blue lines that tie it to the red truck, tan dog, and the blue plaid upper background. Because of the value and texture similarities between the gray plaid tires and the olive plaid background, the truck was outlined in a lighter plaid to sharpen the tire edges. A single row of red in the border feathers the edge of the big red truck.

Hook tan dogs and orange cats with a variety of camel and rust wools. Combine light, medium, and dark values to indicate highlights, shadows, and texture.

little
andy

I wanted to hook a group of rugs with meaning as well as good looks.

1986 another novice hooker joined the class I was taking with Mary Paul. She stunned the rest of us by returning the very next week having completed an 18" x 26" rug depicting her cat. At that the rest of us slackers sat up and took notice. Those of us who had been working on a mere footstool cover all fall term sensed that we needed to get ourselves in gear.

I chose to hook the Quail Hill Designs pattern *Ewe and Lamb*, a medium-sized rug with a ewe and lamb encircled by a vine and a few simple flowers and leaves. Carolyn, who had already sent me a Puritan frame, encouraged my new enthusiasm by sending me a strip cutter to help me deal with the poor-quality, hard-to-cut background fabric I was struggling with.

By the end of the spring term I had completed that rug. It has been on my kitchen floor for 13 years, and in spite of four cats and four dogs it looks as good today as it did when I finished hooking it.

Gradually I moved from hooking commercial patterns to reproducing antique designs, hoping to discover how to obtain the look of age that I love. When I had hooked enough rugs to minimally cover my softwood floors, I felt I was ready for a new challenge. I wanted to hook a group of rugs with meaning as well as good looks.

EVER SINCE THAT TIME I HAVE BEEN ON A JOURNEY. I began it where I live now, in Kenne–bunkport, Maine, as I designed rugs depicting the historic homes here. Then I moved back in time, hooking rugs documenting my childhood memories. From there I traveled farther back, illustrating the stories my dad told about his childhood. In all, from the time I finished *Ewe and Lamb*, I have hooked almost 100 rugs.

In this book I hope to share with you, as I do with my students, what I have learned about hooking technique, color, and primitive rug design. Beginning rug hookers should consult

In this book I hope to share with you what I have learned about hooking technique, color, and primitive rug design.

one of the fine texts listed on page 56 for basic hooking instruction. On page 55 there's information on the tools and finishing method I use in my rugs.

My rugs will teach as much as my words—the captions that go with the rug photographs will explain in detail the actual creative process behind each rug. You'll find that I often admit to pulling out and rehooking a section, or reconsidering my color and design choices. That's how I learn about color, design, and the statement a rug makes—and how you'll learn, too.

My purpose in the chapters to follow is to stimulate how you think about design and color. I want to encourage you to start a journey of your own that will result in hooked heirlooms prized by future generations for the memories they evoke.

primitive
old rugs & new

Primitive rug hooking developed in the northeastern United States, eastern Canada, and the Maritime Provinces in the mid-1800's. Early rug hookers drew original designs on burlap grain sacks, cut worn clothing into narrow strips, hammered a nail into a piece of wood that fit into the palm of the hand, and bent and filed the nail into a hook shape. By holding the fabric strips under the burlap foundation, and using the hook to pull loops of the fabric through the holes in the burlap, a rug hooker was able to create a rug with a lush pile on top. That same process, but using a variety of backings and store-bought hooks, is the one used by present-day rug hookers.

THE EARLY HOMEMADE DESIGNS ARE THE RUGS I ADMIRE MOST. They are usually simple, straight-forward, and often naively drawn. Men and women drew and hooked the things they knew and cared the most about: pets, farm animals, flowers, homes, ships. Geometric quilt designs were also favorites. Manufactured patterns did not become popular until after the Civil War; they were more de-tailed and lacked the inaccurate idiosyncrasies of the earlier home-drawn patterns. At the time, people liked a more professional look, but the more crudely drawn rugs tell us more about the subject and the rug maker than their neatly and accurately drawn descendants.

Today there are pattern makers who specialize in producing the simple, naive designs of those early rug hookers. I, like many rug hookers, have hooked these patterns after making modifications to them, such as removing the spots from a Dalmatian to make it look like a Labrador retriever. The advantage of

modifying a printed pattern is that the pattern maker has done the designing for you. The pattern's attractive composition is what drew you to it. All you have to do is make minor changes. You can concentrate your energies on the challenges of color planning and hooking.

Very early rug hookers used the limited variety of fabric colors that were available to them, such as beiges, browns, and grays sparked with red from long johns and greens probably dyed from vegetable matter. Today's rug hookers can create an attractive primitive rug with that limited color palette by using neutral hues, plus red and green. It may be more interesting to hook with a variety of fabrics, but when this country was young, fabric was scarce and floors were cold. The objective was to use what you had and get the job done.

When I was first hooking, I purchased neutral wools and dyed the light gray and beige fabrics the colors I had trouble finding in

fabric and thrift shops. I soon settled on favorite rusty red, old gold, Colonial blue, and olive-green formulas. With them I could go from one pattern to the next with the same fabrics. As time went on, however, my rugs began to look like a matched set. They reminded me of those coordinat-ing materials available in home decorating departments—they were a little too similar for my taste. The antique rugs I admired contained variations of the same few colors. The variations produced a richer, more complex look. I determined that the way to achieve that look was to collect small amounts of a variety of wools in my favorite hues. I love brick-reds, old golds, olive-greens, gray-greens, bottle-green, blue-gray, Colonial teal, and plum. From that point on I have not dyed wool for my own use.

By using small amounts of a variety of these colors, I can replicate the look of antique rugs the way they appear today, their previously

Rug hooking can be relaxing, therapeutic, and rewarding. The challenges, be they from designing, dyeing, or planning a pattern's colors, are there when you are ready.

bright colors soiled and faded. Just as I love the look of an old blanket chest, with its scars and faded paint, I love the look of an aged primitive rug. An antique rug on my floor would be damaged by the hard use it would be subjected to by my family and pets. So in order to have the look I like without the guilt resulting from abusing an expensive antique rug, I hook primitive-looking designs in dull wool.

ALL I HAVE LEARNED ABOUT THE DESIGNING AND COLORATION OF PRIMITIVE RUGS I have passed on to my students. I believe in learning new skills in stages. That is why I advocate kits for beginners. All the planning and the gathering of materials are done by the instructor, which leaves the beginning hooker free to concentrate on technique.

For each session I teach, I design a beginner rug, an example of which is my *Lamb in Orchard* rug. I was teaching an adult education class and the husband of one of my students had signed up for the course. I knew the couple owned two sheep, Chopin and Amadeus, who resided in a barn at the edge of an apple orchard. So Chopin (or is it Amadeus?) became the subject of that session's beginner rug.

All of my beginner rugs are small (approximately three square

feet), yet large enough to be used as a floor covering and simple enough to be completed by a beginner in six weeks. In designing this rug I had to decide how complicated I wanted to make it. I could include some or all of the following: the two sheep, the barn and corral, the white Colonial farm house, the apple orchard. Trying to replicate the look of rugs drawn by early primitive rug hookers, and keeping in mind that large shapes are easy for beginners to hook, I drew a single, large, simple sheep and as much of an apple tree as it took to communicate what was to me the most novel aspect, sheep living on the edge of an apple orchard.

After I teach my students the basic technique of hooking I teach them color planning. Color planning is a complicated skill that all hookers continually strive to perfect. It is important for the student to be able to accurately explain the desired result to the teacher and for the teacher and student to determine how to achieve it without too much trial and error.

The neutral plus red and green color scheme common to antique primitive rugs is acceptable to most of my students. In *Lamb in Orchard*, the sheep, tree trunk, foliage, and apples were perfectly suited to that color selection. Notice how I made those big red apples large enough to be visible on the tree and put two fallen apples on the ground to provide my pupils with more opportunity to use red.

Once a beginner knows precisely the look he or she is after and has had some experience choosing wools that achieve that look, she is ready to learn to dye. It is easy for beginning dyers to get carried away dyeing pretty colors, forgetting which colors they need to hook the rug they envision. Many of my students never learn to dye. Dyeing useful colors can be difficult, messy, and time consuming. It is not for everyone, so I encourage beginners to learn only as much as they want to know. Rug hooking can be relaxing, therapeutic, and rewarding. The challenges, be they from designing,

These basic approaches to primitive hooking are what I teach my students and what I will teach you in the pages to come.

Lamb in Orchard
24 1/2" x 17"
Single-thickness, hand-cut wool strips hooked through burlap.

PHOTOGRAPH BY DAVID ALLEN.

THE LAMB'S BODY was hooked with a variety of oatmeal and light brown wool tweeds, which give it texture and dimension. The head and legs were hooked in a single fabric to give them a contrasting texture and to make them cohesive, maximizing their visibility. Whenever you want a shape to hold together, hook it in one fabric. A solid fabric usually results in a more clearly defined shape than an area hooked with a tweed or plaid.

The tree foliage and apples are a variety of greens and reds, giving the impression of highlights and shadows. The different fabrics actually enhance each other, making my favorites more noticeable.

Using a variety of fabrics in a background has lots of advantages. Less of each fabric is required; the background is more interesting to hook and to look at; darker or lighter values may be used for outlining to highlight or soften an object's edge; and lint, soil, stains, and replacement strips are less obvious. Keep background values similar to avoid a wormy effect.

A single row of red in the border brightens the rug and increases the prominence of the red apples. Any color used in the border highlights objects in the center that are also that color.

dyeing, or planning a pattern's colors, are there when you are ready. That's what has kept me an enthusiastic hooker for 14 years.

I ALSO USED THE *LAMB IN ORCHARD'S* COLOR SCHEME IN *BESS AND THE MOCKING BIRD*, a small table mat I designed for a one-day workshop. My first dog, Bessie, was accosted by the same mockingbird every spring while I walked her through a park along Atlanta's Chattahoochie River. The

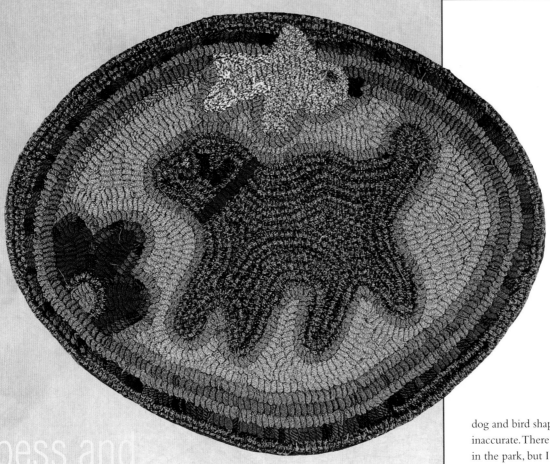

bess and
the mocking bird

Bess and the Mocking Bird
18" x 14"
Single-thickness, hand-cut wool
strips hooked through burlap.

PHOTOGRAPH BY CHRIS SMITH.

ALTHOUGH MY DOG BESSIE was solid black, I hooked her using a charcoal tweed to make this mat look faded and worn. Over the years dark and bright fabrics fade, and light and bright fabrics darken with ground-in dirt. To give your rug the look of age, avoid using very dark, very light, or very bright fabrics. Use medium-dark, medium, and medium-light values instead. Colors can still be strong, but instead of being pure they should include some dark neutral soil, so to speak. Use tweeds to replicate the uneven pattern of fading and soiling.

Because there was not much value contrast between Bessie and the background, I outlined her in a brighter, solid version of the background tweed fabric. The most visible parts of tweed fabrics are their light threads. They catch your eye and soften the edges of tweed objects on tweed backgrounds. In order to make it clear where the object begins, use a row of solid fabric to separate the two tweeds. Using a solid material in the flower increases its visibility in this largely tweed mat.

dog and bird shapes are simple and inaccurate. There were no flowers in the park, but I needed a place to use some color, so I included one. The striped border has the same purpose—to add color to the design. This is a simple mat but, like seeing a photograph of a long-forgotten event, it brings Bessie and Atlanta to mind.

With both of these rugs I did what the early rug hookers did—I selected favorite animals and familiar scenes for a pattern, drew them in a simple style, and then used a seemingly limited yet evocative palette to hook something useful. These basic approaches to primitive hooking are what I teach my students and what I will teach you in the pages to come.

there's a positive side to flaws

When I show people my rugs, I have a habit of pointing out all the flaws in them. I estimate that 90 percent of my rugs have a fault I would correct if I were hooking those same rugs today. Here's what I mean: I went through a period of cutting my wool strips too wide (approximately 1/2") and hooking rows too far apart. The rugs with this wool are matted now with continual use and the strips are easily removed by my puppy, Mocha. Then for a while I hooked with cashmere, but found that cashmere mats down badly, too. When I first tried mixing background fabrics, I ended up with too much difference between values, which gave my rugs a wormy look. And in trying to duplicate the patchy backgrounds I had seen in old rugs, I initially chose fabrics too far apart in value. My patches were bold when they should have been subtle.

I COULD GO ON AND ON LISTING THINGS I WOULD DO DIFFERENTLY TODAY, but the truth is I love each of those flawed rugs. Some of them remind me of what was happening while I hooked them, and all of them document the development of my hooking skill. At times I have felt like I had arrived—I had figured out how to get the perfect look—and then almost immediately I would be inspired to proceed in another direction toward a new vision. The lesson I learned was that flaws have value in a rug, and while I may not want to duplicate those flaws in future projects, I wouldn't remove them in past ones.

The attractiveness of flaws extends to other things besides rugs. After my husband and I had purchased our present old house in Kennebunkport, Maine, my husband hired a contractor and told him to "fix it up." The 100-year-old clapboards were rough with the layers of peeling old paint, and Michael wanted to replace the boards with smooth new wood. Meanwhile, I visited a Society for the Preservation of New England Antiquities (SPNEA) property and bought a booklet on restoration. It said that one of the most common mistakes people make is removing the flaws that attracted them to a building in the first place. Fortunately, we retained the old clapboards and we adore the look of age that their bumpy paint imparts.

I believe this principle applies not only to houses, but also to people and rugs. It is our idiosyncrasies that endear us to others. At an auction, which primitive rug do you think will get the most attention, the Santa rug with the mile-long reindeer, or the one with the accurately proportioned reindeer?

A FLAW IN THE LANDSCAPING OF MY HOUSE'S YARD and the way my husband attacked the problem inspired me to hook a rug. In a sense this rug depicts how most people deal with what they perceive as unsightly errors that in truth lend character. Our home is our first old house, and shortly after we bought it we visited Colonial Williamsburg and met a woman who spent a lot of time teaching us about restoring and decorating such a house. The first time she visited our home she mentioned that the two trees in the front yard were too close to the house.

Downed Trees
12" in diameter
Single-thickness, hand-cut
wool strips hooked through
burlap.

PHOTOGRAPH BY CHRIS SMITH.

BECAUSE OF THIS MAT'S SMALL SIZE, it was hooked mainly with solid fabrics and with more contrast than is required when elements are larger. Solid fabrics produce stronger, more cohesive forms than tweed fabrics, which result in softer, less defined areas. A strip of house color separates the house and barn roofs.

downed
trees

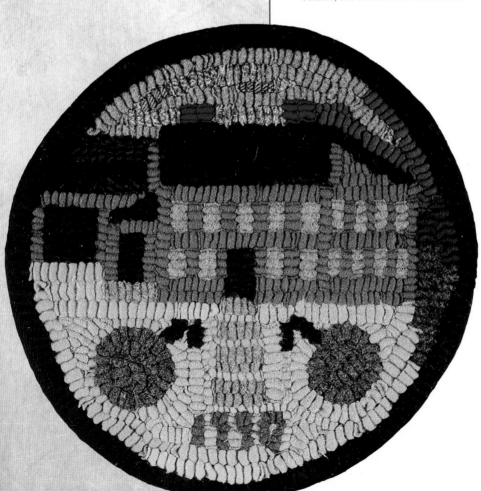

The lesson I learned was that flaws have value in a rug, and while I may not want to duplicate those flaws in future projects, I wouldn't remove them in past ones.

That was all the encouragement Michael needed. He never did like those trees. He slipped outside and headed toward the chain saw in the back of our carpenter's truck. The next sound the decorator and I heard was the buzz of the saw, followed by the crack of the first tree hitting the ground. Before we could rush outside, the second tree had fallen.

The woman tried to maintain her composure and help me maintain mine, not realizing how accustomed I was to my husband's just-do-it personality. To commemorate the event and thank her for her help, I designed and hooked a round mat showing our house and the two fallen trees.

I drew the front of the house straight on, attaching a straight-on view of the side. Angling the roof to accurately depict the gabled roof line seemed complicated, so I drew a straight line from the top of the roof in the front on down until it met the back wall of the house. The two fallen trees, granite walk, back step, and the date were all that were necessary to record the day for posterity and fill the circular mat. When that decorator and I talk, we still laugh about the day the trees came down. I wonder if we would if she didn't have that mat to remember the occasion.

FAMILY MEMBERS HAVE ALSO RECEIVED RUGS THAT CAN CALL TO MIND A MEMORABLE TIME. Several Christmases ago I wanted to hook a small gift for each of my three sisters. This was close to the time I had hooked the oval *Bess and the Mocking Bird* mat. I decided to hook all the mats the same size, thinking that that would be a manageable amount of work

and that the mats could be used as chair seats or table mats. I wanted to save time by hooking the same pattern three times. The three rugs would share neutral hues but would be distinctive in other, stronger colors.

The result was the *House with Fence* mat. The mat depicts a bird, cherry, flower, fence, and a saltbox house. I chose a saltbox because its shape and simplicity were compatible with the available space. I reasoned that I could personalize the houses using the colors found on each sister's real house. I'd change the bird species and flower to be compatible with the different house colors. All the mats would have dark backgrounds to highlight the light picket fence.

I enjoyed hooking the mats because each was small and simple enough to be a quick project. One of my earliest original rugs was an anniversary gift for my parents that, while also small, was in no way simple, a flaw that I learned a great deal from.

I DECIDED TO MAKE A RUG I COULD FINISH IN TIME FOR THEIR ANNIVERSARY, one that depicted their home. My parents live in a Cape Cod house with an addition on the back. I like to avoid using perspective in rugs in an attempt to achieve a naive look and avoid hooking converging

House With Fence
18 ¹/2" x 15"
Single-thickness, hand-cut
wool strips hooked through burlap.

PHOTOGRAPH BY CHRIS SMITH.

THE FRONT AND SIDE OF THE HOUSE are defined by using two values of oatmeal. The lighter value appears closer to the viewer because it's on a dark background. Hook a pattern's more prominent elements in a value that contrasts with the background value. The fence would have appeared closer to the viewer if it had been hooked in the lighter oatmeal.

The flowers, stems, and leaves were hooked in leftover reds and greens. Gold plaid windows are warm and inviting, as is the red plaid brick walk.

house
with
fence

58 Puritan Road
26" x 19 ³/₄"
Single-thickness, hand-cut
wool strips hooked through burlap.

PHOTOGRAPH BY CHRIS SMITH.

INSTEAD OF A SOLID, WIDE BORDER FOR THIS RUG, I wish I had made the center area larger, with 1" top and side borders. Wide borders can occupy a large percentage of the area of a rug and dominate it. The bottom border could have been wider and included all of the printing.

Although grass is bright, it should be hooked with grayed or browned greens (you might call them dirty greens) to decrease its prominence. In most rugs, grass forms the background and thus should not stand out. Because I hooked the grass in this rug with a dirty green, the green house, shrubs, garden foliage, and tree top in the foreground could then be hooked in brighter greens, allowing them to be focal points.

Small items, such as this scene's birdbath and lawn swing, are more visible when hooked in solid fabrics in values that contrast with the value of their backgrounds. Note the dark green foliage behind the birdbath and the darker green grass beneath the lawn swing. You probably didn't notice the change in background fabric until I pointed it out, but it helped you see what was going on. The various parts of the swing are hooked in different fabrics to tell them apart. I rearranged the spots on the dog to make him show up on the background and to define his ear.

58 puritan
road

diagonal rows. Almost immediately I knew that the addition was going to be trouble. To show the front and side of the house was going to take up a lot of room, yet everything was going to have to be small in order to include the garage, three windows and a door on the front of the house, and a chimney and windows on the side. Then I recalled the row of cedar trees on the side of the house; I would have to include them. Then I'd have to include the shutters, and the peaked roof over the front door, and the shrubs Mom and Dad always kept neatly trimmed. To soften the garage door, I would have to add the fence, and the arbor over the gate, and of course the potted geranium I gave them after my trip to California.

Naturally my design wouldn't be complete without picturing Mom, Dad, and Dad's basset hound, Dean-O. My mother is an avid gardener, and it occurred to me that a picket-fence border and my mom's lovely back-garden flowers would be striking design elements. And I couldn't leave out the row of forsythia bushes, the birdbath garden with the magnolia tree, the lawn swing, and the picnic table and benches.

Are you beginning to see the problem? I managed to draw all this in a simplified manner, becoming more enthusiastic by

> If ever there was a rug
> that could have used a simple border, this was it,
> but emotion outweighed artistry,
> just as it often did
> in the hooked rugs of the 1850s.

the minute, but as soon as I had the design on burlap and began to hook I knew I had a problem. It's hard to make a 3"-long dog look like a spotted hound using $^1/_4$"-inch wide strips of wool. The windows were so small I couldn't define even 4 glass panes (there were really 12). Windows without panes don't look much like windows to me, but I had a deadline, so I just cut my strips narrower than normal.

Here's the caveat I learned designing and hooking this rug: Small things are difficult to hook with wide wool strips. I could have more easily hooked a larger rug and not had to struggle to make each small motif look like what it was. It was a lesson I have learned the hard way more than once.

SEVERAL YEARS LATER I WAS LOOKING FOR ANOTHER SPECIAL ANNIVERSARY GIFT FOR MY PARENTS. I decided to hook the house on Morse Street where my sisters and I grew up. It was a two-family, two-story house with a mansard roof. This time I decided I'd profit from past experience and design a larger rug to accommodate more details of family memories, such as the time my dad fell off a ladder while helping my grandfather paint. I could show Grampa Noden on a ladder painting the front of the house (he was

a house painter by trade) and my grandmother watering her favorite plant, Solomon's seal.

The problem was that while I had increased the dimensions of the rug I had also increased the number of details in it. As one warm memory evoked another I yearned to include yet another in the pattern. After all, as long as I had included my dad and grand-parents in the scene, I couldn't leave out my mom. I could show her trimming the hedge that bordered the front of the property. I would have to include the detached garage with the two paved tire tracks separated by grass and the apple tree that overhung the garage from the rear. We kids used to climb up onto the garage roof from the apple tree, driving Grampa Noden crazy. Then there was the lawn swing Grampa sat on while reading stories to my sister Bev, and the grapevine clothes yard Bev fell out of, breaking her shoulder blade. Of course I had to include my grandfather's many gardens, which reminded me of the baby blue jays Mr. Bivens returned to their nest after they

had fallen onto the flagstone path.

See how much fun designing your own rugs can be? I hadn't thought of these things in years, and I wondered if my parents realized how important all of these memories were to me. If they were as excited as I was, my gift would be a treasure. It certainly was to me.

As you can imagine, I encountered all of the same problems hooking this rug that I had encountered hooking the previous anniversary rug. I bravely eliminated some of the gardens, then broke down and added one of us girls on the wooden stilts my dad made for us. I got so carried away reminiscing that I decided on a border listing some of the memories I couldn't include. If ever there was a rug that could have used a simple border, this was it, but emotion outweighed artistry just as it often did in the hooked rugs of the 1850s. A simple border would have better suited such a complicated rug, but the imperfection provides insight into the personality and mindset of the creator.

Rug hookers hone their skills

> Give each rug your best effort
> and move on
> to the next one.

102/104 Morse Street
37" x 27 ¹/₂"
Single-thickness,
hand-cut wool strips
hooked through burlap.

102/104
morse street

PHOTOGRAPH BY CHRIS SMITH.

Hooking a background in different fabrics that are similar in value allows objects to be outlined in values that can sharpen or soften their edges. The house in this pictorial was hooked in old gold instead of its actual color, Colonial yellow, to give the rug a softer, older appearance. Remember that colors become soiled and faded with the passage of time.

The people were drawn simply, without detail; they don't even have eyes. But characteristics such as clothes and hair style can help viewers identify people. White hair, a V-neck house dress, and black shoes make it obvious to those who knew her that the woman with the watering can is Gramma Noden. The man in the white coveralls and hat is obviously a professional house painter—Grampa Noden.

I wish the border edge were straight, but I am glad I hooked the lettering in a plaid. Parts of the plaid are the same value as the border, which obscures parts of the letters and softens them. If I had wanted them to be easy to read, I would have hooked them with a solid fabric.

with practice. Give each rug your best effort and move on to the next one. You will learn from your successes and mistakes. If you don't like something you did, don't do it again. The flaws that are obvious to you won't seem important when your floors are covered with a history of your rug hooking development.

combining beauty & substance

When my husband and I moved into our old (but new to us) house in Kennebunkport, Maine, it had no wall-to-wall carpeting, and I realized this was my opportunity to use hand-hooked rugs as floor coverings throughout my home. The predicament was that I knew I would have to have a lot of them hooked by the time we moved in or my husband would rush to the store to purchase an instant solution to the problem of cold, slippery floors. I scanned my primitive catalogs, ran through the inventory of rugs I had already hooked, and ordered patterns for most of the major bare spots. I began hooking floor coverings for the house while we were still in Atlanta and continued as soon as I had recovered from the stress of cleaning up after four months of having carpenters, painters, and electricians in every room. Within about a year most of the obvious bare spots were covered, and I was feeling inspired to hook rugs that were a bit more than attractive floor coverings.

AS I WALKED MY DOGS THROUGH OUR HISTORIC NEIGHBORHOOD, I began to think about creating a group of rugs honoring the wonderful houses there. New people were moving into some of them and changing them forever. I decided it would be fun to document them so that when I'm 85 I could look at my floors and reminisce about the 1990s.

Right away it occurred to me that most of these Kennebunkport houses were two-story white Colonials. I decided to begin with the most unusual house in the neighborhood, the Captain Lord Mansion. The Lord mansion is a three-story yellow Colonial with a cupola. It is now used as a bed-and-breakfast establishment. It has a small porch outside the front door, a flagpole mounted under a second-story window, and leaded glass surrounding the front door and middle second-story window. I sat across the street from the house with a pad of graph paper and drew the house, carefully counting the graph's squares and lining everything up to make sure I didn't get into the same fix I had gotten into with that first anniversary rug I had hooked. In that rug I had to eliminate one window and resort to meager $1/4$"-wide shutters. This time I was determined that there would be room for everything, from windowpanes to siding between windows.

In spite of its bold presence, and aside from its leaded glass and cupola, this is a pretty ordinary house. I decided to draw the leading and the six-sided cupola accu-rately. I couldn't figure out how to deal with the flag, so I eliminated it. After cramming so much detail into those anniversary rugs, this rug was going to be medium-sized and picture only the house.

I realized that that simplicity meant this rug was going to be very yellow, and I like red. I noticed an inconspicuous double row of bricks edging the shrubs. By emphasizing them I could repeat the red of the chimneys at the bottom of the rug.

When I got home I cleaned up my drawing and enlarged it, covered the drawing with veiling (not netting, which is too course to transfer the design adequately), traced the drawing with a broad-tip marker, and transferred the drawing onto Angus burlap by placing the veiling on top of the

Captain Lord Mansion
38 ¹/₂" x 34"
Single-thickness, hand-cut wool strips hooked through burlap.

PHOTOGRAPH BY DAVID ALLEN.

A TWEED WAS USED TO HOOK THIS HOUSE'S shutters to reduce the contrast between them and the old gold siding. The windows were hooked in a gray-blue and beige tweed so it looks as if they were reflecting the color of the sky. The dentil molding at the roof edge and under the cornice is indicated by checked fabric.

Use patterned fabrics to indicate details too small to be hooked individually. You may have to try several fabrics before you achieve the proper effect, but the interest they add is worth the effort. Brick-red was used in the border and lettering to contrast with the green in the shrubs and background.

burlap and retracing the black lines. I left plenty of margin, anticipating a border based on the leading pattern in the windows.

I like old-looking rugs, so I hooked the house in old gold instead of yellow. My house has dark floors and I prefer low-contrast rugs for them because they are mildly inconspicuous. When I enter a room I prefer to see the furniture first, then the curtains, then the walls, and then the rugs. For me, high-contrast rugs are jarring. Some rug hookers feel that because early primitive hookers sometimes used brightly colored fabrics, today's rug hookers must also, but that is not the look I like. I want my rugs to look 100 years old right now, (After 100 years even bright colors will have dulled.) I hope someone is still enjoying my rugs long after I am gone, but I don't see the logic in foregoing certain pleasures today in the uncertain hope of benefiting future generations. In terms of

their color, all of my rugs look as good today as they did when I finished hooking them, despite years of use. If they are properly taken care of, I don't anticipate their color to significantly deteriorate during my lifetime. Part of my confidence is based on my use of commercially dyed wools.

The greatest hooking challenge in the Captain Lord Mansion rug was the shrubbery. It was an even greater challenge than the leaded glass. Shrubs are often sculpted into symmetrical shapes that look severe when hooked. The naturally shaped bushes beside the porch are much more attractive to me. Having had the same difficulties with the shrubs in the anniversary rugs, I have since eliminated shrubs from subsequent rugs.

As my hooking was proceeding I added the date that the house's construction began and also the name of the first owner. I had designed wide borders inspired by the leading pattern in the glass, but later realized the center of this rug was making enough of a statement. A simple border was called for, and because the center is dominated by straight lines, a softly flowing border would create balance, softening the mood of the rug. I settled on a gently scalloped edge with a two-row border. As is common in primitive rugs, the outer row is

Some rug hookers feel that because early primitive hookers sometimes used brightly colored fabrics, today's rug hookers must also, but that is not the look I like. I want my rugs to look 100 years old right now.

Josiah Linscott House
35 ¹/₂" x 24"
Single-thickness, hand-cut wool strips hooked through burlap.

PHOTOGRAPH BY DAVID ALLEN.

THE PROTRUDING PARTS OF THIS HOUSE were hooked in light oatmeals, causing them to advance toward the viewer. The roof was hooked in a gray plaid to mimic the texture of gray shingles.

The different values in checks and small plaids, like the ones used to hook the vine's stem, cause the vine to alternately appear and disappear, making it visible but not as obvious as the flowers and leaves. This stem is a bit light but it gives the vine form and works well with the leaves and the red flowers, which are close in value to the background. If the leaves and flowers were lighter, they would compete with the house for attention. Either the plants or the house should dominate, and it is appropriate that the house does.

the darkest color in the rug. I chose chimney-red for the inner row to add pizzazz and to separate the dark border from the dark background.

AFTER HOOKING THIS, THE MOST COMPLICATED HOUSE IN THE NEIGHBORHOOD, I hooked the simplest house. The Josiah Linscott house is a white Cape Cod with gray pilasters, windows on either side of the front door, and an overhang above the front door. Once again I sat across the street from the subject of my rug with my pad of graph paper and quickly sketched the details. Notice there are no shrubs.

I knew right away that just as the complicated Lord mansion needed a simple border, this simple rug would need a more complicated border for balance. I was looking around for ideas and

josiah
linscott house

Gideon Walker House
45" x 27"
Single-thickness, hand-cut wool strips hooked through burlap.

PHOTOGRAPH BY DAVID ALLEN.

THIS RUG NEEDS MORE COLOR CONTRAST. I wish the background had been hooked in a medium-dark old gold to contrast with and emphasize the purple lilacs. Because I had only two oatmeal fabrics, I hooked the center protrusion and ends of the house in the lighter value. The recessed extension on the left and the front of the main house on both sides of the protrusion are hooked in the darker value.

gideon walker house

found one in a book on scheren-snitte (scissors cutting). The tree of life border adds softness and color to a rug otherwise composed of stiff geometric shapes.

BY NOW I WAS ENJOYING MYSELF AND HAD IDENTIFIED MY NEXT SUBJECT, the Gideon Walker house. I noticed it because our house is the Daniel Walker house. I surmise, based on the dates of the houses, that Gideon had been Daniel's father or uncle.

I particularly liked the chimney on the small addition. The protruding two-story addition sheltering the front door also appealed to me. I sketched the house as I had done previously, eliminating all the shrubs except the lilac bushes (for which I have a weakness). This house sits atop a bluff overlooking the mouth of the Kennebunk River, hence the wave border and corner stars. This was an attempt to be creative and add some history and personality.

Soon after I hooked this rug the house was sold and the new owner made some modifications. I brought the completed rug to the first class of the fall session. One of my students said, "Hey, that's my house." Since then, that student has become a proficient rug hooker and has told me that the back of the house may have originally been the front, and that it used to be known as the little red house. Think of all of the design possibilities here. One rug could picture three versions of the same house.

Hooking the houses in my neighborhood gave me a chance to capture my town's past. In the future I would learn to design rugs that preseve not only a building's shape and size, but also its personality.

more than meets the eye

After I had been hooking house rugs for about six months, I attended a Quail Hill rug hooking workshop here in Maine, directed by Marion Ham. Before class started, students were invited to wander through Marion's home to see the hooked rugs that covered her floors. As I descended the front stairs, I saw her *Your House Rug*.

IN THIS RUG, A DEPICTION OF THE FRONT AND ONE SIDE OF HER HOUSE was hooked into the upper right-hand quarter. Under the house, filling an equal amount of space, was a collie. A horse the size of the dog took up the lower left corner, and a vase of flowers occupied the upper left corner. Three different flowering vines separated the four major items, one on each end of the rug and one down the center.

When I saw that rug, I said to myself, "I get it." Although the rug's house didn't really look like Marion's actual house, I recognized it as being her house. I assumed that she owned a dog and a horse that were important to her. I didn't know the significance of the flowers and vines; they could have represented her large garden or were just added to provide pattern and color. I saw this rug only briefly, but it inspired me to decrease the significance of the houses in my rugs and add elements that impart important information about the structures and their inhabitants.

As part of Marion's workshop we were given the opportunity to draw an original rug. During a lecture I doodled a drawing of our house, the Daniel Walker house, with our Labrador retriever, Bessie, and our cocker spaniel, Andy, lying side by side in front of it. I included our outdoor cats, Kitty and Dusty. Dusty is lying on his back ready for a pat, his normal response to our approach. Kitty is looking alert and defensive as is his habit. Our indoor cat, Molly, is in the second-story window.

Huge elm trees used to line the streets of Kennebunkport. Most of them are gone now, victims of Dutch elm disease. You see one to the left of our garage. Narrow branches don't really appear abruptly atop sturdy trunks, but the trunks are sturdy and the branches thin. The trees are twice as tall as the house and I didn't have room to include the middle portion of the tree.

In the back of our house are a cherry tree and an apple tree. I decided to take advantage of the opportunity to avoid drawing more tree trunks and show only fruit and foliage. The cherry tree looks like it is growing out of the chimney. Oh, well! Notice the leaves are characteristic of the trees they represent. The elm leaves are long, thin, and pale green, the cherry leaves are larger and darker green, and the apple leaves are rounded and a soft gray-green.

We are proud of our 200-year-old windows—you can tell that by the way I outlined each pane of glass. I also included Bessie's tennis ball, a compass indicating true north in relation to front of the house, and a forget-me-not flower in memory of Bessie, who had just passed away.

Marion's rug inspired me to decrease the significance of the houses in my rugs and add elements that impart important information about the structures and their inhabitants.

Daniel Walker House
54" x 37"
Single-thickness, hand-cut
wool strips hooked
through burlap.

PHOTOGRAPH BY DAVID ALLEN.

daniel
walker
house

I USED A CHARCOAL TWEED TO REPRESENT BESSIE'S SALT-AND-PEPPER muzzle, paws, and leg fringe. Andy's smooth back was hooked with a single solid fabric. His curly face, ears, side, and legs were hooked in different values, giving them pattern and texture.

The house was hooked with a single fabric. Dark lines separate the sections of the structure. I could have used three values of the house color, the strongest of which would have gone on the house (the most prominent building), the middle one on the recessed connector to the barn, and the weakest one on the distant barn. The parts of objects that are close to us appear stronger in color than the parts that are farther away. Colors close to us are brighter and white is whiter.

Different fabrics similar in value were used to hook the background. Curved objects were concentrically outlined until outlines met. Avoid hooking background in straight lines. Curves are more pleasant to look at and produce a flatter rug.

Note the red line in the border, a welcome contrast to all the green. A row of tan-and-red plaid is a soft bridge between the tan background and the red border row.

I lengthened and broadened the brick walk to give me an opportunity to use more red. Between the neutral animals, our khaki-drab house, and all the foliage, the rug was looking very green. Green's complement, red, added balance. A simple four-row border was the finishing touch.

My design for this rug is random in a fairly organized fashion. This is a function of my personality. My philosophy is that hooking is a bit like handwriting: Some people are naturally neat and some people aren't. As long as writing is legible, we tolerate and even expect uniqueness. I tolerate and expect to see differences in each student's hooking, within certain parameters. Just as handwriting must be legible, loops must be hooked high enough and close enough together to result in a serviceable rug. The only unsolicited advice I give students about design is that they should fill a rug with a close-up of what they want people to see. Unless it has a purpose, background is boring to hook

Drawing a pattern is a bit like cartooning. A realistic portrayal isn't as important as identifying and amplifying unique characteristics.

and to look at. A teacher's job is to help a student achieve the look the student envisions, and it is desirable and natural that each person's rugs will be different.

NOW THAT I WAS INCLUDING MORE THAN JUST HOUSES IN MY RUGS, I could hook the Captain Jefferds Inn, which is across the street from us. The inn, although sprawling and complicated in the back, appears from the front to be a big two-story Colonial. It has a small front porch surrounded by

Captain Jefferds Inn
34" x 24 ¹/₂"
Single-thickness, hand-cut wool strips hooked through primitive linen.

PHOTOGRAPH BY CHRIS SMITH.

captain jefferds inn

THE PASTEL PLAID WOOL THAT FILLS THE WINDOWS REFLECTS THE SKY at sunset, adding color and pattern to this rather plain house. Camel wool was used to hook skin, and a gray/tan/off-white tweed was used for the stubble on Warren's chin. Don's white jacket is oatmeal outlined with gray to define the sleeves and front edge. Green fabric surrounds the brown trousers.

The check pants and plaid shirt are surrounded by solid versions of the background tweed to sharpen their edges. I had to experiment until I found a check fabric that, when hooked, resulted in the correct size of checks for Don's pants. Too-small checks can create a tweed effect.

The tea towel was hooked with a blue-and-white plaid wool. The bluer strips were used to hook the edges, leaving the whiter strips to fill the center.

I rearranged the basset's spots save for the distinctive white tail tip. It is surrounded by dark background to make sure it can be seen. The large shaggy dog's hip and head are defined by a dark value. Light values make him appear shaggy. Notice that his curly fur is hooked in random C shapes.

A teacher's job is to help a student achieve the look the student envisions, and it is desirable and natural that each person's rugs will be different.

the same leaded glass the Captain Lord Mansion has. The inn is white with a centered dormer and a small front porch. The front of the inn alone would result in a rug much like the Gideon Walker house. Including the innkeepers and their pets would express the personality of the inn and make an interesting and unique rug.

I decided to place the inn in the center of the rug, drawn in the same fashion as the houses in my previous Kennebunkport rugs. I ignored the leaded glass. This inn has a casual feel to it that fussy leaded glass would not communicate.

The innkeepers, Don and Warren, are as tall as the inn so I could hook some detail into their faces. Don and Warren are opposites, and their looks are expressive of their personalities. If they were not interesting, I would not have made them so large. Warren, on the right, cooks the breakfast, indicated by the apron, mixing bowl, and spoon. (If I want to get my message across, I can't be subtle.) Don used to serve the breakfast, so I dressed him in a white jacket and draped a tea towel over his arm.

I draw a human figure simply. I start with an oval head, then draw one side of the body. I give it a short neck, a shoulder that extends beyond the head, a sausage arm, a torso a little shorter than

the arm, and a sausage leg. Then I proceed up the other side of the figure, finishing at the neck. You can bend arms and legs in any direction, just like a sausage.

Once these basics are in place I add simple clothes and mitten-shaped hands and shoes. Shoes viewed straight on are half circles, flat side down. Viewed from the side they are a toe and a distinct heel.

Don is an easy-going fellow with a tousle of white hair. His head is an oval with C-shaped ears, round eyes, a straight mouth, an inverted U-shaped band of hair bridging his ears, and a stray lock of hair across his brow. That's not a complicated drawing, yet it is accurate and expressive.

Warren is more serious. He is balding, wears horn-rimmed glass-

My philosophy is that hooking is a bit like handwriting: Some people are naturally neat and some people aren't.

es, and has a fashionable stubble of beard. His head, ears, and mouth are the same as Don's, but I added glasses as well as a beard line that runs between his ears starting just above his mouth. I hooked his beard in a tweed that gave the appearance of gray stubble.

Don and Warren's three dogs are also present—Brother, the shaggy dog; Jenny, the small dog in the center; and Mabel, the basset (Mabel tended to wander, so she is leashed). The Captain Jefferds welcomes dogs traveling with their families, hence the pets.

Dogs and cats can be drawn in profile with large oval bodies. Dogs have round heads, long or short snouts, and pointed or drooping ears. Cats have round heads and pointed ears. Both can have sausage legs and tails. Zigzag the edges of the body to indicate shaggy fur, and add eyes and a collar for definition. You can refer to pictures to hook different breeds of dogs, but try not to get too technical. Remember the look of those early rugs.

I completed the design with the date and name of the house's original owner. I thought splitting the name was clever when I did it, but I wish now I had printed it uninterrupted in a wider bottom border.

Drawing a pattern is a bit like cartooning. A realistic portrayal isn't as important as identifying

Snug Harbor Farm
57" x 26"
Single-thickness, hand-cut
wool strips hooked through burlap.

PHOTOGRAPH BY DAVID ALLEN.

I USED ALL OF MY OATMEAL LEFTOVERS TO FILL THE DIFFERENT SECTIONS of this string of attached buildings. Fabrics were chosen for the different parts without regard to which sections were closer. In a few places I used gray lines to separate sections.

The trees were hooked with leftover greens and golds. The hues were placed in patches so the lighter, brighter fabrics are on the right (sunlit side) and the medium values are on the left. The different greens could have just as well been used randomly resulting in the same texture as in the lamb's body in *Lamb in Orchard*.

I never should have hooked the sky with such a green-blue fabric. There was already plenty of green in the rug. But not wanting to change the sky, I eliminated the grass in front of the buildings and used a brown tweed there for dirt and for contrast. Notice how the speckled hens are surrounded by a dark solid to separate them from that tweed. If the horizon had been plum and the sky a grayed blue, the foreground could have been green, which is a good background for rust pots, oatmeal sheep, a brown tree trunk, and speckled hens.

From the beginning I knew this rug was going to be largely green and white. I was depending on the brightly colored flowers to give it punch, but as the hooking progressed I knew I needed to add red for balance. I added a rust vine with red flowers to the sides and top.

and amplifying unique characteristics. First think about what is unusual about a house, person, or animal, then think of how you can visually represent that quality. Don't be too subtle.

I TRIED TO PORTRAY A LOCAL FARM'S UNUSUAL QUALITIES when I hooked my next rug. Snug Harbor Farm is a rambling row of small white buildings. I threw caution to the wind, discarded my graph paper, and drew a disproportional string of misshapen rectangles and triangles representing the farm. The farm sells plants, and from the beginning I wanted to include them in front of the shed on the left. As I had done in the

**Primitive artists know what
makes a cow look like a cow.
They know which characteristics to
emphasize to make each species
instantly recognizable.**

Gideon Walker rug, I also wanted to indicate the farm's proximity to the ocean, so waves run along the bottom of the rug.

The animals actually graze in back of the buildings, but as I hooked I sensed a need for the warm feeling their presence would impart. The dimensions of the rug were limited by the size of the backing, so I had to squeeze as many creatures as I could into a narrow strip in front of the buildings.

Notice the simple shapes of the animals. If I am unsure how to draw an animal I consult photographs or examine early or contemporary primitive art. Primitive artists know what makes a cow look like a cow. They know which characteristics to emphasize to make each species instantly recognizable. Primitive paintings also contain a lot of technical information, like how a horse hooks up to a wagon. And there are mistakes in primitive art as well, which are fun to incorporate into rugs. I have seen odd-looking interpretations of how seated people look that are much more fun to see than accurate renditions.

If I were to draw *Snug Harbor Farm* again, I would add lawn,

place one of the farm's peacocks on a roof, and have the sheep and goats grazing in a corral that's behind the buildings. There are many other features of the property that would be good motifs for a rug. Just the fact that I am thinking of them shows how that long-ago look at Marion's rug influenced my perspective on designing rugs. It reminded me that, just like with the childhood home I had hooked for my parents, it is the personal associations you have about a building that make it unique.

Nathaniel Lord 1799 Hou
34" x 26"
Single-thickness, hand-cu
wool strips hooked throu
primitive linen.

PHOTOGRAPH BY CHRIS SMITH.

nathaniel
lord
1799 hous

don't ignore the obvious

Sometimes something other than its inhabitants makes a house unique. One of the most extraordinary things I saw after moving to Kennebunkport was the huge American flag our neighbor hangs on a rope strung between a tree and the roof of his house. I spent years wandering around my neighborhood trying to think of ways to give all of its Colonial houses personality so I could hook them into interesting rugs, yet I never gave that flag a thought. Luckily it finally dawned on me that I should never ignore the obvious.

WHEN HUNG VERTICALLY, THE TOP OF MY NEIGHBOR'S ENORMOUS FLAG is even with the top of his second-story windows, and the bottom is a only a foot or two from the ground. I imagined that years ago it had been strung between two tall elms on either side of the front yard (I could see the remains of stumps in the lawn).

In drawing this pattern I strung the flag between two elms. I drew the house in a relaxed fashion, not as precisely as in my graph paper drawings, yet not as casually as I did with the buildings at Snug Harbor Farm. I made sure the trees towered over the house. I carefully observed the Victorian hood, which I wanted to include because it was the most memorable feature of the building (the house dates from 1799, and all its other characteristics are of that period).

I love fences, so I included the one that's in front of the house. I think fences are wonderful design elements, and I include them whenever I can. They provide strong pattern and direction, and different styles are indigenous to different areas of the country. Beside the fence I hooked the granite pillar that, in the past, had marked the corner of the street.

THIS RUG'S FLAG STRIPES, FENCE, AND DOOR OVERHANG WERE HOOKED IN A LIGHTER OATMEAL VALUE than was the house to bring them forward on the dark background. The foliage was hooked in different greens and golds to give it texture and highlights. A royal blue and black check outlines and defines the edges of the foliage. If the foliage had been hooked with lighter greens, outlining would not have been necessary.

The star portion of the flag was hooked with the same blue-and-white plaid fabric as was used in the tea towel in *Captain Jefferds Inn*. This is another example of using a fabric's pattern to indicate details too small to hook with 1/4" to 3/8" strips. The perfect plaid would have had more blue in it.

The tree trunks are a gray tweed. Tree trunks are gray when they are dry and dark brown when they are wet. Using a tweed or small plaid results in a barklike texture.

When you are working on a complex design
and the proper placement of motifs is important,
draw them on individual pieces of tracing paper.
That way you can move them around
until you like their arrangement.

THIS RUG WAS EASY TO DESIGN AND HAS A LOT OF PERSONALITY. Now I wondered what other rug design I could think of that could tell a story or convey a mood. Then I recalled Christmas in Dock Square.

Dock Square is Kennebunkport's business district. Its 25 or 30 small shops are frequented by tourists during the summer. Most of the stores close during the winter months, but they are all open during Christmas Prelude weekend. There are lights, garlands, and wreaths decorating all of the shops and inns, and candles flickering in the windows of all the old houses.

Prelude weekend begins with the lighting of a huge Christmas tree set up in the middle of Dock Square. The tree is decorated with lights and colorful lobster buoys. A wooden lobster tops the tree. During the lighting program elementary school children sing carols accompanied by a crowd of residents and visitors. At the end of the program the tree lights are lit and the children sing "It's Beginning to Look a Lot Like Christmas." The ceremony is particularly wonderful when it snows.

I have thought about hooking Dock Square in the past, but the square is really a triangle with the most significant buildings on all three sides. The Christmas tree provides a focal point. Depending on my point of view, I could have

chosen as a background the old Colonial Pharmacy, Alisson's restaurant, or the Bookport.

I chose the Bookport. The building was a rum warehouse during the early 1800s when great sailing ships were built on the Kennebunk River. It has a cupola with a wooden bird perched on it and two large windows framing a display of lights strung in the shape of a Christmas tree.

Photos reminded me exactly how the buildings on that side of the square look. The leftmost building has a gabled roof on one end of it with a flat-roofed extension linking it to the Bookport building on the right. I copied the door and window placement and added shutters to the second story for pattern and color. The Bookport, with its door and two windows on the first floor, its large center second- and third-story windows, and its cupola, didn't need much modification. I only ended up shortening the cupola to maintain the rectangular shape of

Sometimes something other than its inhabitants makes a house unique.

the rug. In the center of the square, beside the tree, is a statue of an eagle surrounded by a small stone wall.

This rug was more of a challenge to me than I expected. I had to place the tree and statues on a plane that lay in front of two buildings and their arrangement of windows and doors. To make it clear what was going on, I had to be careful the items in front didn't obscure important parts in the back. I reverted to graph paper to draw the buildings. Next I drew the tree, making sure that the portions of windows and doors at its sides were large enough to be recognizable. I placed the monument between the two buildings and had it appear to touch the Bookport so no sky would show between them. In a confusing scene, avoid small patches of things. Don't confuse the viewer with insignificant, avoidable distractions.

With the basics done, it was time to decorate the scene. This was not going to be a large rug, so I knew the details would have to be simple and easy to identify. Wreaths could be simple circles with bows composed of a rectangle between two C shapes. The shop windows on the left could be defined by a row of garland decorated with bows. The tree of lights in the Bookport windows would have to become a green Christmas tree in order to be seen.

Dock Square Christmas
31 1/2" x 22"
Single-thickness, hand-cut wool strips
hooked through burlap.

PHOTOGRAPH BY DAVID ALLEN.

There are always wooden lobster traps under the community tree. On this rug they became striped boxes decorated with ribbon and bows. The buoys on the tree are large in order to have stripes on them. The stripes are important because they signify who owns the lobster trap to which the buoy is attached. Each time a lobster man goes to sea to pull his traps, he attaches one of his buoys to the top of his boat so it is obvious that he is pulling his own traps. I added bows to the tops of the buoys.

Two animals remained to be hooked, one the simple lobster on the top of the tree, and the other the eagle on the pedestal. Lobsters are complicated, but almost anything can be simplified. A long, thin rectangle formed the lobster's

THIS SETTING'S SNOW WAS HOOKED WITH OATMEAL, NOT WHITE, FABRIC to give the rug the look of age. Gray oatmeals look whiter than beige oatmeals. The rug has both gray and beige in it. The night sky was hooked with a saturated blue-gray solid, the faded version of midnight-blue.

Two green plaids created the Christmas tree. The sheltered boughs on it were hooked with the greener plaid; the snow-covered branches with the beige-green plaid. Windows were filled with a gold-and-oatmeal plaid for warmth and sparkle. Note the row of red in the border.

dock
square
christmas

> In a confusing scene, avoid small patches of things. Don't confuse the viewer with insignificant, avoidable distractions.

body; a short rectangle placed perpendicularly across one end of the body made the tail; and quarter-circle sausage shapes emanating from the center of the body became the claws. The eagle, in contrast, was hard to hook. I reduced it to a round head on a larger oval body with a wing shape on either side.

To make it look like it was snowing, I drew circular snowflakes in the sky and in front of the buildings and covered all horizontal surfaces with a one-row layer of snow. Just before finishing the rug I added Bessie and Andy gazing in awe at the spectacle.

This is a pretty complex small rug. When you are working on a complex design and the proper placement of motifs is important, draw them on individual pieces of tracing paper. That way you can move them around until you like their arrangement, then tape them down and trace everything onto a fresh piece of paper, eliminating anything extraneous. Now add details to the comprehensive drawing. If the drawing gets messy as you add details, redraw the parts you like, eliminating the residue of ideas you tried and rejected. A fresh drawing will help you evaluate your design accurately.

Emma Rose Salt Marsh Farm
45" x 35"
Single-thickness, hand-cut wool strips hooked through primitive linen.

PHOTOGRAPH BY CHRIS SMITH.

THE HOUSE, WHICH USED TO BE COLONIAL YELLOW, is hooked with two values of old gold to separate the sections without outlining them. The texture of the shake shingle roof is represented by a brown-and-tan plaid. The road is hooked with the same brown plaid as the roof, as if it were dirt. The lawn close to the house is hooked in a dirty green to cause it to recede. The foreground pasture is hooked in patches of more saturated greens and green tweeds to make it advance.

The sky appears blue even though it is hooked with a beige tweed that includes a bit of blue. Blue is a strong color that advances. In rugs with lots of sky, use a fabric that is barely blue or a mix of fabrics so the sky won't dominate the rug. The blue marsh water in the foreground should probably have been hooked with several solid fabrics and the inlets concentrically outlined.

emma rose
salt
marsh
farm

point of view

In planning the design of a rug, look at your subject from different points of view. Point of view was what I wrestled with in my next rug, *Emma Rose Salt Marsh Farm*. I wanted a viewpoint that was artistically pleasing. But I also wanted it to accurately communicate the mood of the scene.

FOR SOME TIME I HAD BEEN THINKING ABOUT HOW TO DESIGN AN ATTRACTIVE RUG based on the Emma Rose Salt Marsh Farm. The farm is the perfect subject for a primitive rug. First, the old house and its attachments are stunningly attractive to anyone interested in old buildings. To make the scene even more appealing, the house overlooks a long stone wall separating the other side of the road from a grassy hill and a seemingly endless salt marsh. The hill is populated by sheep guarded from coyotes by a large white dog.

The farm's owner raises chickens and keeps bees. She also raises a rare breed of sheep for its wool. As a matter of fact, the farm is named after the woman's favorite sheep, Emma Rose. Emma Rose was born early and had to be kept in the house until the weather improved. When she returned to the flock she was not accepted by the other animals and has been pampered by the family ever since.

Driving by, you approach the scene from the road that separates the farm from the pasture. My

planning questions started from that point. Should the road be a strong horizontal line running straight across the rug? That way I could draw the farmhouse straight on, but then the horizontal road would attract more attention than either the farm or the sheep. I could place the road diagonally, but then I would have to fit the long farmhouse and attachments into a triangular space. That would be awkward and not characteristic of the straightforward simplicity of the scene and the family.

After thinking about this farm off and on for years, it finally dawned on me that the solution was to pretend I was standing on the far side of the marsh looking up the hill at the sheep and the house. As the road is flat, it would be barely visible, and I could present the house head on looking its best. I drove out to the farm and parked along the side of the road. While I was sitting there sketching the buildings in a relaxed style, the sheep turned around to watch me, so I sketched them, too.

When I got home I got out fresh paper and redrew the buildings and the huge hemlock. I

Elizabeth Perkins House

added a dirt road and dirt driveways, a post-and-wire fence paralleling the road, and the sheep facing the viewer as they graze on the edge of the marsh. I had trouble drawing the water in the marsh but decided not to worry too much about it. I also included a shed and the old family cemetery. Patches across the pasture indicated undulating high and low spots and bright and shaded areas of grass. And I didn't forget the farm family's chickens or bees.

At the time I was happy with my design, and I love the rug it became. However, if I were drawing this rug today, the farm would be smaller and drawn in Snug Harbor Farm style. I would include the stone wall snaking across the rug from one end to the other. The pasture would occupy a

greater portion of the rug, more accurately portraying its prominence.

HERE IS ANOTHER EXAMPLE OF THE DIFFERENCE POINT OF VIEW CAN MAKE. The Elizabeth Perkins House in York, Maine, is a gorgeous red two-story Colonial situated along the banks of the York River. There is a large attractive extension on one end. The house belongs to the York Historical Society and the grounds are open to the public, so I was free to stroll around it snapping photos.

In planning the design of a rug, look at your subject from different points of view.

As I wandered out back I saw that the house was situated on a high bluff at a spot where the river narrows. Beyond the house and to the left I could see the unique profile of Sewall's bridge spanning the narrow river. Viewed from behind, the house is a series of multiple peaks, windows, and chimneys. Tall trees line the top of the bluff.

When I designed the Elizabeth Perkins House rug I placed myself in a boat on the river looking up at the bluff. From this vantage point I could see the structure's complicated pattern of

Rock Haven

rectangles and triangles as I looked between the trees spaced evenly along the top of the bluff. To the left of the house the river disappears behind the historic bridge.

This house is situated in much the same spot relative to the York River as the Gideon Walker house is to the Kennebunk River. Do you suppose this house also originally faced the water and not the land? A rug portraying the Perkins house from the back tells much more of a story than one showing it from the front. Being able to incorporate the bridge is a

I added roses to the pattern for color because pictorials are often dominated by neutral colors.

big plus. It documents the possible historic significance of the house.

ANOTHER ARTIST GAVE ME A LESSON ON POINT OF VIEW WHEN IT CAME TO MY OWN HOUSE. One year there was a fair on the town green and one of the vendors was offering to paint watercolors of people's homes for a fee. We asked her to paint our house, and when she came to take photos to work from she persuaded us to let her paint the back, not the front, of the house as we expected.

Admittedly the front of our house is not particularly interesting or unique, and the back is the same as the front—with the exception of a single-story ell on one end and a huge flower garden. The artist stood in the far corner of the lot and photographed the back of the house with the garden in the foreground. What an interesting painting that made. The garden added color, complexity, and insight into the personality of the current owner.

Personality was what I wanted to include in a pattern for a friend's rug, but in the end it was the point of view that made the design distinctive. Last summer a friend asked me to design a rug featuring her family home, Rock Haven. She sent me photos of the way it used to look and the way it

**When we look at a scene,
we focus on the parts of it that interest us.
When we draw rugs we want to communicate
what we perceive—not necessarily what is really there.**

looks now. I asked her to think of anything significant, like pets or people, that I could include to add personality to the scene, but nothing seemed particularly important to her. She was even ambivalent about whether the house should be portrayed in its current or past state. I knew where the house was and drove over to look at it to see if I would be inspired.

The house is on a peninsula. It faces the ocean, and an inlet and marsh are in back. Behind the house you can see a little bit of water, then marsh grass, then a thick area of tall trees on the right. To the left, water and marsh lead to a bridge. What a nice background for a rug. But how was I going to indicate that the house is on a peninsula?

The answer was to imagine myself on the ocean facing the peninsula. I pretended I could position my boat so I could see choppy ocean water, then a horizontal band of the small, smooth black stones the ocean heaves up onto the shore. I would barely be able to see the road separating the rocky beach from the front of the house. I could add a stand of beach roses just beyond the black stones for color (rose and green) and softness. I sketched the background while I was at the house, then went home and, on a fresh piece of paper, drew the house from the photos and added the background and foreground.

I added those roses to the pattern for color because pictorials are often dominated by neutral colors. Houses are seldom colorful and lawns, shrubs, trees, and soil are all green and brown. I like my skies grayed because bright blue skies can take over a rug.

When we look at a scene, we focus on the parts of it that interest us. When we look at a house, we don't pay attention to the lawn or the shrubs or the sky. We might not even remember the trees. When we draw rugs we want to communicate what we perceive—not necessarily what is really there. One of the ways to give items the appropriate amount of weight in a design is to adjust their color. A bright green tree is more prominent than a dull one. A grayed blue sky is less prominent than a bright blue sky. By adjusting color, you are applying the same filter to your subject that your mind applied when you viewed it. As an artist, you are sharing with the viewer your impression of the scene, not an accurate factual representation.

To make sure there would be enough color in my friend's rug, I colored a copy of the design. I increased the red in the rust roof, deepened the brown of the weathered shingle siding, and brightened the beach roses. The orange in the rusts and browns balances the blue in the gray-blue sky and water. If the rug needed more color, I could change the season to fall and add reds and golds to the trees in the background on the right. A row of rust or red along the inside edge of a border adds a substantial spark to a rug, and I knew that if, after the majority of the rug was hooked, the design needed more red to balance the greens, a row could be included.

inspiration from other artists

Since I began hooking rugs I have tended to focus on a style or subject matter until I am bored with it or inspired to experiment with another. I started with animal rugs. They were easy to color plan because the central figure was a neutral color. I avoided florals for a long time because they were difficult to color plan, but eventually I became intrigued by the challenge. For a while I hooked only geometrics, and for years I tried to duplicate the look of antique rugs. I hooked light backgrounds, then dark backgrounds, and even started a pattern company (Port Primitives) and hooked the designs I planned to sell.

EVERY TIME MY FOCUS CHANGES MY ENTHUSIASM IS REVITALIZED. The change can be motivated by something I see along the road, at class, or in a book, or by something that happens, like moving into a new home. My most recent change in focus was inspired by two rugs I ran across in an antique store. They bore the initials of Barbara Merry, a Maine rug hooker I had read about and whose style I have admired. In addition to being fascinated by their design, I was intrigued by the quality and variety of fabrics and the hooking technique.

The rugs were hooked on a burlap base with a variety of fabrics, such as coarse cottons and thready, woven blends. There was a good deal of linear patterning—house siding, roofs, lawns, and fields of crops were hooked in alternating rows of two or more colors. The plain borders were subtly striped in single or double rows of different fabrics close in color and value. All of the fabrics were hooked in a double thickness, done by folding the strips in half lengthwise while hooking them. These rugs were fascinating.

Noel
22 ¹/₂" x 15"
Double-thickness, hand-cut wool strips hooked through primitive linen.

PHOTOGRAPH BY CHRIS SMITH.

MY OBJECTIVE IN THIS PIECE WAS TO PRODUCE A LIVELIER RUG; my strategy was to accomplish that by using fabrics with greater contrast than I normally use. The oatmeal snow is accented with royal blue instead of taupe, which would have been my usual choice. The bright sky is defined by wavy lines hooked with gray-blue and lavender solid fabrics. The side and front of the house were hooked in wools of different colors, not just different values of the same color.

**Every time my focus changes
my enthusiasm is revitalized. The change can be
motivated by something I see along the road,
at class, or in a book,
or by something that happens,
like moving into a new home.**

I am not in the habit of buying antique rugs to use as inspiration. They are much too costly. Years ago I had discovered that I could not duplicate the look of a rug I had seen without having a photo of it to refer to. As hard as I would try, I could not remember the combination of details that produced the look I was after. But even with a photo to refer to when choosing fabrics, I would jump to inaccurate conclusions that resulted in a look unlike the original rug. I would compare the fabrics I had chosen with the colors in the photo and be surprised at how far off my choices were. One time a friend lent me her antique rug so I could make a reproduction for her. Having the rug to study and refer to was a tremendous advantage. There is nothing like a life-size model to compare your work to and to inspire you.

I absorbed as much about the two Barbara Merry rugs as I could, then went home to search for the magazine article I had that

pictured several of her rugs. However, the pictures were so small that I could not see the magnificent variety of textures and colors the rugs probably contained. I had noticed the price on the smaller of the two store rugs and was beginning to rationalize how I could justify buying them both.

The medium-size rug was divided into quarters with scenes portraying each of the four seasons in the quadrants. A border surrounded each scene and the words "Four Seasons" were hooked in the bottom border. The other rug was larger and was a farm scene. Together the rugs contained all the elements of pictorial rugs: a variety of buildings, trees, skies, water, snow, people, and animals— enough ideas to keep me busy for years.

I managed to delay my trip back to the antique store for a little over a week. When I returned, both rugs were still there and they were even more interesting than I remembered. The dealer's best price was my upper spending limit

and I returned home with them.

The next few days were spent rolling and unrolling them— inevitably I'd unroll a rug, concentrate on one detail, roll the rug up, then later think of something else I needed to study. Eventually I draped one of the rugs over an old drying rack so I could observe it frequently.

I wanted to try hooking with double-thickness strips, so I gathered my thinner wools together and cut a few 1/2" strips. I folded the strips in half lengthwise with my left hand as I hooked the material through the backing with my right. I found it was much easier to have the fabric's fold on the right and the cut edges on the left. By holding the fabric between my thumb and forefinger, I could tell when the cut edges were aligned, but it was almost impossible to line the edges up when the fold was on the left. Left-handed persons will probably find the reverse to be true.

Hooking with doubled strips was fun. They pulled through the primitive linen easily and seemed to pop to the surface like I've always imagined narrow strips do for tapestry hookers. I drew a small rug to hook with doubled strips that included snow, clouds, a pine tree, a simple house with smoke streaming from its chimney, and a large cardinal standing on a pine bough in the foreground. I used a

**Clipping softened the surface and
gave the rug a matte finish.
In addition, the tops of the unclipped
double-thickness loops had a shine
I had never noticed before.**

Neverdun Farm
24 ¹/₂" x 21"
Double-thickness, hand-cut wool strips hooked through primitive linen.

PHOTOGRAPH BY CHRIS SMITH.

THIS RUG IS A BIT BUSIER THAN THE NOEL RUG. The lawn in front of the house and barn was hooked in alternating rows of khaki and blue-green solid fabrics. Notice that the brown house is subtly striped in a brown solid and check. The crops in the field are rows of different greens separated by rows of dark brown plaid soil. The lettering's background is a soft neutral, the same fabric used in the house. For an antique, make-do look, repeat fabrics when possible.

variety of thin and thick wools. They were all easy to hook doubled and I was pleased with the look of the doubled loops. However, the design of the rug didn't please me. My objective had been to simplify the house and ignore realistic proportions. But the house seems too small. To get the look I was after maybe everything in the rug needed to carry the same weight.

The primitive paintings of Clementine Hunter have also been inspiring me lately. Clementine uses a wide brush and paints simple, expressive images often depicting a chain of events. Sometimes she uses two horizontal planes. Forms in both the foreground and background planes are large enough to be easily drawn with enough detail to make them recognizable. Sizes are not relative. Large items are simplified and reduced.

NEVERDUN FARM WAS MY NEXT ATTEMPT AT ACHIEVING A NEW LOOK. I wanted to give all components equal weight, use a greater variety of fabrics and colors, and end up with a rug that looked old. I drew the house, barn, and trees on a distant plane, simplifying them and making them large enough to be easily hooked with wide strips. Then I drew the people on the near plane, making

them large enough to be easily recognizable. The shed is drawn the same size as the barn even though the shed, being so much closer to the viewer, should actually appear much larger than the distant barn if the rules of perspective were employed. The dog is small in relation to the people but fits nicely in the available space. Did you notice the diagonally striped sky? That was the best way I could think of to hook rain.

When I showed this rug to my students, one of them told me

Primitive rugs are composed of a few large shapes hooked in a fairly limited number of wools. Folk art paintings are often composed of many small items in a variety of colors and patterns.

that this is not Neverdun Farm. The mailbox with that name on it actually belongs to another farm obscured from the road, and the field is not connected to the brown house and barn. I had driven by one rainy day and noticed people dressed in bright slickers working in the field. I thought they would be a good subject for a rug. I just assumed the field they were in and the mailbox's name related to the house across the road. I will have to include that unfortunate bit of information on the label I attach to the back of the rug.

The style of the Neverdun Farm rug looks more like folk art than primitive to me. Primitive rugs are composed of a few large shapes hooked in a fairly limited number of wools. Folk art paintings are often composed of many small items in a variety of colors and patterns. I like the design of this rug, but it is a little bright with a little too much contrast, and it is a bit too neatly hooked.

WHILE I WAS IN AN EXPERIMENTAL MOOD, I NEEDED TO DESIGN A RUG TO TAKE TO A WORKSHOP. The instructor was going to be Jessie Turbayne, a woman who makes her living repairing old rugs. I knew she has seen a lot of old rugs and hoped she could give me advice about hooking a clipped-pile rug.

I wanted to hook the Salem Cross Inn located in Brookfield, Massachusetts. The property had been in my dad's family for more

than 200 years. The current owners had converted it into an inn and restaurant. The inn is a two-story farmhouse with an extension linking it to the barn, which is now the restaurant. A roof supported by large white columns has been added to the front of the barn providing cover for guests entering and leaving during inclement weather.

I searched through pictures of old rugs for inspiration and soon focused on a series of simple rugs that contained only a single large building (and sometimes a tree) and large printed letters identify-

ing the building. The simplicity of these designs seemed appropriate for a clipped-pile rug, as I assumed the pile would produce a fuzzy image. I drew my pattern, transferred it to primitive linen, packed up my thinner wools (thinking that hooking with doubled strips would enhance the soft look of a clipped pile), and headed to the workshop.

At the workshop I learned that there are two ways to achieve a clipped pile. You can hook nor-

Sometimes I forget that in order to grow I must not be too quick to abandon a new vision.

mal-height loops and clip each one individually with your scissor tip, or you can hook higher loops and clip several tops off at a time holding the scissor blades parallel to the surface of the rug. I elected to clip the loops of my rug one at a time and found that clipping softened the surface and gave the rug a matte finish. In addition, the tops of the unclipped double-thickness loops had a shine I had never noticed before.

Unfortunately, despite my design decisions and my new hooking technique, the primitive look I had hoped for did not

Salem Cross Inn
34" x 23"
Double-thickness, hand-cut, clipped and unclipped wool strips hooked through primitive linen.

PHOTOGRAPH BY CHRIS SMITH.

salem
cross
inn

materialize. I found I could hook as much detail into a clipped-pile rug as I could a looped-pile rug. Maybe heavier-weight wools would have resulted in more primitive, less defined shapes.

As I hooked and clipped I realized my lettering was not going to have the primitive look I wanted, either. I began to worry that my plain background would be boring even if I used patches of closely related fabrics. Rather than struggle to achieve a different look, I reverted to a look that had been successful. I added a leafless tree, a rainbow, and a dog sitting beside the Salem Cross sign. A wide bottom border contained the dates during which my father's relatives owned the farm and the year it became the inn.

I wish I had switched to heavier-weight wools and kept to my original plan. Sometimes I forget that in order to grow I must not be too quick to abandon a new vision. If the result is not superior, I can always revert to tried-and-true methods. Most of the time a new approach becomes an element of my style, and achieving a new look, whether good or only fair, is stimulating and rewarding.

ALTHOUGH THE FRONT OF THE INN and the columns are bright, the rest of the rug is more peaceful than the Neverdun Farm rug. That's because there is less contrast in values among the background fabrics.

Different sections of the house are hooked in different oatmeals, the closest being the brightest. The background is hooked with a tan, green, and off-white windowpane plaid. The fabric's tan panes are about 1" to 1 1/2" square. Windowpane plaids make wonderful flecked backgrounds.

The sky is defined with charcoal-navy drifting clouds, the same fabric as is found in the bottom rainbow stripe. Note the subtle striping of the border.

Some of the loops in this piece have been clipped and some have not. The clipped loops have a frayed, soft look and the unclipped ones resemble pebbles.

telling tales with wool

Hooking a rug of an old house is a way of preserving a structure's history. But hooking can also preserve a family's history. *The Salem Cross Inn* was, in a sense, a preservation of my family's past, but I was soon to find another source of inspiration that accomplished that in a deeper, richer way.

MY DAD GREW UP IN DOWNTOWN BOSTON IN THE 1920S. As a teenager he and his family moved to the city's suburbs, close to where he and my mom eventually settled and raised our family. Like many people who live on the outskirts of big cities, Dad and Mom rarely went into town. When my husband and I lived near Boston we loved going into the city to shop and dine, and we often invited my parents to go along. As we'd pass streets, my dad would point out the different places where he had lived, and, encouraged by Michael and a glass of wine at lunch, he'd describe his childhood memories of the city.

My husband and I love listening to the stories our elders tell us. You can learn as much about the history of the homes in our town at a holiday cocktail party as you can by reading a historical society booklet. As we approach our 60s the memories of an older generation are becoming dearer. And as the neighbors next door prepare to move into a retirement home we realize that we better listen closely to their stories of

days gone by while we still have the opportunity.

It occurred to me that my dad's stories would provide subject matter for an interesting series of rugs that would warm our floors and our hearts and maybe keep his stories alive for another generation or two. What a great idea!

I told my dad about my idea and started quizzing him about his youth—like the time his mother sent him to mail a letter. She gave him two cents and told him to stop at the drugstore, buy a stamp, then mail the letter. To her surprise he returned home with the two pennies, explaining that, since no one was looking, he was able to slip the letter into the mailbox without the stamp. His mom explained the problem to him and sent him back to buy the stamp and wait for the postman to empty the box so my dad could

add the stamp. Dad's clever, cost-saving idea had boomeranged.

As we reviewed the details of the scene I grabbed a piece of paper so I could draw a rough sketch. He had told me that they were living at 31 Massachusetts Avenue at the time. I knew Massachusetts Avenue was lined with multiple-story brick and brownstone buildings, so I asked him how many stories his building had. He told me six. I drew a tall rectangle, and as I did I asked how many windows were on each floor on the front of the building. He told me three. I drew three windows across each of the five upper floors. Then I asked him about the doorway. He said the door was wood, painted beige or some other light color, and that the doorway was recessed. He remembered walking up two or three steps within the recess to the door.

Hooking with double-thickness wools produces loops that form a mosaic pattern. Each loop is like a bead.

I drew the door atop three rectangular steps set into a larger rectangle (the recessed area). The steps were draw in a pyramid to create the illusion of depth.

Once Dad got talking he gave me lots of information. Dad explained that he lived on the basement level and their apartment didn't have front windows. I drew the side of the building in perspective so I could include his apartment. He remembered that the alley between his building and the one next door was paved with cobblestones. He remembered that his mother hung her laundry in a fenced clothes yard on the roof of their building. Gradually the details of the two buildings took shape.

Next I asked him where the mailbox was in relation to the buildings. He told me it was on the corner next to another building. I drew a large mailbox standing on the sidewalk, not the smaller version that used to be mounted on a utility pole, because in the rug it was going to have to be large enough to have "U.S. Mail" on it—I knew I had to make it as clear as possible what was going on. Then Dad and I went over other aspects of the scene, such as whether the buildings were red brick or brownstone, what the sidewalk was made of, and whether there were any trees.

When I got home I redid my sketch. I added sheets pinned to a clothesline on the top of my dad's building. The wash had to be made up of large, easily identifiable items because it would have to be small and there was going to be a fence in front of it. Clothespins were important because they would confirm a viewer's suspicion that that was wash hanging. I drew the sides of the buildings facing left so the mailbox on the right would be more prominent. Then I drew a little boy, shorter than the mailbox

Two Pennies Saved
31" x 23 ¹/₂"
Single- and double-thickness,
hand-cut wool strips hooked
through primitive linen.

PHOTOGRAPH BY CHRIS SMITH.

two
pennies
saved

THIS RUG CONTAINS A BRIGHT SKY SUITABLE FOR A HAPPY CHILDHOOD MEMORY. Light and dark aspects of the scene were hooked in brighter or duller hues, respectively. For example, recessed areas of the buildings are darker than protruding ones. Two thin dirty purple wools, each folded in half lengthwise, were used to hook the shadowed sides of the buildings.

The brick sidewalk is a loosely woven rust-and-navy plaid. The flowers in the corners were hooked with brightly colored leftovers. Note the striped side borders, subtle but more interesting than a plain border.

The hardest parts to hook were the boy and the drugstore door. The door color needed to be subtle yet distinguishable from the building and mailbox, and the black-and-gold apothecary symbol had to be visible on it. The boy's clothing had to be masculine and show against a variety of background fabrics. Furthermore, his arms were important, so his forward arm had to be hooked in a second value to distinguish it from his torso. When an object has many backgrounds, it can be difficult to find a fabric that shows up well on all of them. Change your color and value until the object can be seen, especially if it is important. "U.S. Mail" is hooked in a plaid to give it the washed-out look of stenciled lettering.

but tall enough to be able to drop a white rectangular letter into the box. My dad always wore a cap, and pictures of him when he was young often show him wearing one as well, so I gave this boy a cap and knickers (he often mentioned how much his mom liked short pants on young men and how much he wanted long pants).

Looking through pictures of old rugs helped me settle on three borders that appealed to me. I knew this rug's motifs were largely brick and metal geometric structures and a flowered border would add a colorful, lighthearted touch in keeping with the mood of the rug's story.

I finalized my sketch, enlarged it, then transferred it to veiling and primitive linen. On my next visit I showed it to Dad. He was pleased, but he told me that his apartment was on the other side of the building and that the clothes yard was really in the back.

When I got home, I redrew my pattern with the sides of the buildings to the right. Showing the apartment on the correct side of the building was important. But I left the clothes yard in the front of the building because seeing it well enough to know what it was was more important than having it in the correct location. Now I was ready to hook.

I chose four rust wools, two brighter ones for the fronts of the buildings, and two duller ones for the sides. However, I didn't like the quality of some of the wools I was using, and with so little going on in this pictorial and so many small areas to hook, the quality was a concern. On the bright side, the army-green mailbox looked great, and I loved the wash hanging on the line. I filled most of the window rectangles with mauve wool, but used warm yellow for my dad's apartment windows as

well as for his best friend's apartment and the drugstore.

Those points, however, were quickly turning out to be the only parts of the rug I liked. I disliked the sidewalks' brick tweed and the sky's colors (Blues? Beiges? Plums?) weren't working out, either. My diminishing enthusiasm motivated me to put the rug aside temporarily. After all, this wasn't a rug I was going to finish just to have it over with. The rug was supposed to document a happy memory and I wanted to feel wonderful about it.

It was at about this time that I acquired the Barbara Merry rugs. In reviewing the old magazine article about her rugs, I noticed some of her windows had curtains. I got the *Two Pennies* rug out and added curtains to the windows on the fronts of the buildings (the side windows were too small for them). I knew hooking curtains would be difficult, but after hooking one or two their softness provided the incentive I needed to get the job done. Next I added a few drifting clouds to the sky and began hooking the sky and clouds with a variety of blue wools. Now I was beginning to feel some good vibes. The softness added by the flowing cloud shapes and curtains was turning a cold, angular rug bright, warm, and cheerful.

Up to this point the rug had been hooked with single-thickness strips. I wanted to switch to double-thickness strips but I didn't know whether I should combine both thicknesses in the same rug. Buoyed by my new enthusiasm, however, I tore out the fabrics I was unhappy with and rehooked areas with thinner, tightly woven, double-thickness strips. The tiny windows on the sides of the buildings were now easier to hook, and the disappearing rows

of hooking required to hook the sides of the buildings in perspective were less noticeable, thanks to the doubled wool.

Hooking with double-thickness wools produces loops that form a mosaic pattern. Each loop is like a bead. Lines of single-thickness loops look like rows of ribbon candy. With them it is hard to make a row of hooking end inconspicuously.

Once I was happy with the way the rug was looking, completing it progressed quickly. I replaced the sidewalk brick tweed with something with more personality. I finished the sky with double-thickness loops and added two trees, one to soften each side edge. I printed "Two Pennies Saved" in the top border and "31 Mass. Ave. Boston" in the bottom.

I love the result. It is a cheerful rug that reminds me of my dad and the happy afternoons spent with him.

As I designed this rug I started with the familiar (the buildings), asked questions about basic features (how many windows), included items important to the story or storyteller (the mailbox), and avoided all unessential details. Start with what you know. Once you've begun it will be easier than you think to add elements one at a time, and before you know it your work will be accomplished. Avoid the temptation to include extraneous details that will be difficult to hook and will obscure the point of the rug.

IN DESIGNING A PICTORIAL, THE CHALLENGE is to think of a means of incorporating symbols that convey important information about the story. Your design has to pretty bluntly present key details in order for your viewer to get the

**In designing this rug
I started with the familiar,
asked questions about basic features,
included items important to the story
or storyteller, and
avoided all unessential details.**

point. If you are too subtle the viewer will not even notice you are trying to say something. People are not terribly observant and don't want to ask embarrassing questions. Encourage their interest by giving them enough information in the rug so they have a good idea of what they are being told.

Because there were many more stories I wanted to hook, I decided to take my cue from Barbara Merry and combine four anecdotes into one large rug. I could have divided the space into quarters separated by a grid or vine but decided instead to fill the center of the rug with a large basket of flowers. Then I'd place two memories at each end of the rug, one atop the other. I chose four tales that took place downtown that I felt could be handled pretty simply. They involved my dad, his sister Alice, and his mom and dad. It would be nice to have the whole family represented in one rug. I could write the family name, Evans, as well as everyone's

first and middle names in the bottom border.

In the upper left corner my dad and his sister are skating in the Boston Public Garden near a small suspension walkway. Tall posts and cables support the bridge and give it a distinctive profile. I know from my visits to the garden that there is an island on the far side of the pond with a tree. The tree adds softness and interest to the sky and the bridge's railing is a nice strong horizontal.

Although I'm sure many children would normally be skating on the pond, I placed only my aunt and dad on it, as it was important to give the central characters the spotlight they deserve. I had originally drawn my grandmother sitting on a bench, but when I checked with my dad he said that never would have happened. She spent her time tirelessly helping small children navigate the rough ice and slush along the perimeter of the pond.

I dressed my grandmother in a coat, head scarf, mittens, and

boots. The little boy she is helping is in a jacket and pants with skates and mittens. His hat is perched on top of his head, giving him a pumpkin face. The hat should probably have been more of an inverted U shape to give him a longer, thinner face. Dad and Alice are skating one foot and arm in front of the other for balance. Dad is wearing a jacket, long pants, mittens, and skates. His head and hat created problems, too, for in reality people wear their hats pulled down in back. I also overdid the collars of Dad's jacket and Alice's coat. This made their necks too long. I thought about tearing out and redesigning them but worried that I might create greater problems. Hopefully future generations will get a kick out of my mistake.

The memory depicted below the pond scene is of my dad rolling a tire on hilly Park Street. He didn't anticipate the effects of gravity this day, for as soon as he reached the top of the hill he lost control of the tire and it rolled up on to the hood of a car. The driver was furious and my dad fled, leaving the tire behind.

I drew Dad running just past the crest of the hill. To depict the moving tire I drew a series of overlapping round shapes that I hooked in progressively darker shades of gray. The last tire shape rests on the hood of the car. To

Think of a means of incorporating symbols into your rug that convey important information about the story.

show how mad the man was, I extended his arm out the side window with a large index finger pointed in the direction of the offender.

The third memory I chose was of my dad climbing along the timbers that support Harvard Bridge. The bridge is part of Massachusetts Avenue and is located close to MIT. He climbed along hunched over until he got to the middle of the bridge, then got scared and had a hard time turning around so he could get back to land.

Again we have a fence and a car occupied by a man with a hat. I am not sure exactly what old cars look like, but my memory is that they are rounded with flat backs, like a London cab. Accuracy is not important as long the correct impression is created. The bridge support is curved and water flows beneath. The riverbank at the bottom of this scene ties in well with the scene below, which also

takes place along the river's edge.

The last memory in this rug is of my dad and his dad returning the privately owned playground equipment to the gate house next to the Esplanade, the grassy public land along the banks of the Charles River that is home to the annual Fourth of July Boston Pops concerts and fireworks. In those days neighbors pooled their money to buy the equipment and someone set it out in the morning and returned it at night. Dad told me his father would put the jungle gym on a wagon and Dad would walk alongside steadying it.

I did my best to draw the jungle gym, but in order for it to fit on a wagon it looked too small for children to play on. I showed the drawing to my dad and he acknowledged that it wasn't right but couldn't fix it for me. We decided to make the gym bigger and let it hang over the edges of the wagon.

I have since seen a photo of the two of them transporting the

equipment and it looks exactly like this depiction. I was astounded when I saw how accurate my secondhand portrayal was. Even their clothing was correct. Maybe my father's memory of the event was shaped by the photo, which he may have seen several times over the intervening years.

Besides the playground apparatus the other necessary item to include in the rug was the gate house. I simplified its shape and included its heavy wooden double doors and barred windows. The gate house still exists, although now it is amid a tangle of expressway ramps. Exact detail is difficult to observe at 50 miles per hour, and the important thing is that the idea is conveyed.

As you may have noticed, I placed the more-complicated scenes in opposite corners. That enabled me to combine each of them with a simpler scene that would occupy less space if necessary and result in equal activity on the ends of the rug.

I chose the simplest of the three borders for this complicated rug. As my hooking progressed I widened the top and side borders and added the names of the places depicted.

BORDERS, FLOWERS, AND MORE OF MY FATHER'S MEMORIES occupied the rug that followed *Boston c. 1925.* When Dad was

Boston c. 1925
56" x 26"
**Double-thickness, hand-cut
wool strips hooked through
primitive linen.**

PHOTOGRAPH BY CHRIS SMITH.

young he lived in an apartment next to the Charles Street Jail. He used to stand on a box so he could look out the window and watch horse-drawn wagons carrying prisoners pass through the gate in the prison's brick wall.

What a fascinating sight that must have been for a little boy. I thought for a long time about how to depict this scene. All my dad could see were the brick walls and the wagon disappearing through the gate, and those elements were not going to make a very interesting rug. Soon it dawned on me that what my dad was seeing was not as exciting as what he was thinking. He knew there were bad guys in the wagon and that police with guns ran the prison.

I decided to frame the prison scene with a triple-width window my dad would be looking out of. I have no idea what the real apartment window looked like, but many old city buildings have bay windows. I eliminated the walls between the windows to gain an unobstructed view of the prison.

Remembering again that in a good rug it is more important to depict the impression of what one sees than what one actually sees, I drew the rug assuming Dad could

THE CHALLENGE IN COLOR PLANNING this rug was to integrate the center motif and the corner motifs. It is almost always a good idea to use strong color in the center of the rug and weaker colors nearer the edges, so my first decision was to make the flowers reds, oranges, and purples. I chose golds for the basket and an olive-green and beige tweed for the center background. This was a good decision because green was a logical color choice for many of the corner motif backgrounds, and a common background color would produce a cohesive rug.

The colors of small items, like the hat and clothes in the scene in the lower left, are not as important as the colors of large areas, like the background. Because of their size, small items have little visual impact and mainly need to be distinguishable from their backgrounds.

I feathered the center background fabric into the stronger greens coloring the hill that the car is traveling up. But I wasn't sure about how I would do that scene's sky, so I shifted my attention to the skating scene. There I hooked the water and snow with oatmeals, the people with miscellaneous strong colors, the fence with a strong color, and the winter sky with grays and mauves. At this point it occurred to me to hook the tire scene's sky in blues with snow-colored clouds. Adding blue shadows to the snow would feather the sky into the snow above it.

I thought I could tie the sky in the lower left with the sky in the upper right by hooking the center's small flowers in soft blues to create a blue diagonal. But soft blues bled into the background and outlining them looked contrived. Taupe, probably because of the complexity of the rug, clearly looked best. I completed the rug, making one decision at a time, the easiest ones first, and thus had surprisingly few difficulties.

Charles Street Jail
33 ³/4" x 28 ¹/2"
**Double-thickness, hand-cut wool
strips hooked through primitive linen.**

charles
street
jail

PHOTOGRAPH BY CHRIS SMITH.

The accuracy
of the details
are not as important
    as preserving
the essence
    of the past.

MY JAIL RUG IS BUSIER THAN IT OUGHT TO BE, but it works because of its muted colors. The brightest parts are the "County Jail" lettering and the prisoner's striped clothing, and that's appropriate because that information sets the scene. The iron gate and window bars are other strong elements. Their solid color holds them together, making it easy to tell what they are. They also help set the scene.

The brick wall is a rust-and-gray plaid supplemented by a rust tweed. I began hooking the wall in a solid fabric, but that made it appear too massive. While the wall's massiveness is an important part of the story, I wanted to keep the focus on the prisoner. The plaid fabric accomplishes that.

I got carried away with the stenciled walls and woodwork trim. However, like the brick wall, the walls might have appeared massive had they been hooked with solids.

I first tried gold flowers in the corners of this rug but switched to brick-wall red. Introducing gold added complexity to an already busy rug. With so much going on, a limited color palette was preferable. Vertical stripes in the side borders crowded the busy center section. Horizontal stripes appear to widen the rug and are close in pattern to the lettering. The stripes and lettering become one different pattern instead of two.

see the police unloading the prisoners. I designed the jail, a gray stone building with barred windows, as I recalled it from my days riding the T to work. The important thing is that the viewer knows it is a jail. I have no idea what the real gate looks like, but in order to see inside mine would be wrought iron with spikes on the top and a big lock. The brick wall had to be substantial because this was a large part of the memory.

I dressed the prisoner in a black-and-white striped jumpsuit (that says *prisoner* to me). The policeman is wearing a hat with a large gold star, and his gun is drawn. "County Jail" appears on the side of the wagon and a spoked wheel indicates that the wagon was horse drawn. The driveway may have been paved, but I decided against brick or cobblestone because they would provide little contrast against the red wall and gray jail. Brown earth, with dark and light wheel ruts, would provide a welcome color and texture change. I added a woodwork border to the window and consulted a book on American decorative wall painting for a suitable wall stenciling pattern.

Before I hooked this rug it looked like a lot of large shapes without much detail. That is why I chose such a complicated border. Originally there was a serpentine line with three or four overlapping circles running down the center of the side borders. Striping the side borders horizontally and adding stripes to the bottom border provided uniformity and made the printed letters less prominent. I documented the location in the top border and my dad's nickname, Sonny, in the bottom. My dad's parents and sister were the only ones who called him Sonny. I wonder if any of the grandchildren remember him being called Sonny? They will now.

I DESIGNED ONE MORE RUG DEPICTING MY DAD'S CHILDHOOD memories. One day he told me that during the summers his family would stay with relatives in Granville, New York. They would go by train through a tunnel. Dad, his mother, and sister would stay all summer and his father would return to work in the city on weekdays. I asked him what made summers in Granville such a good memory and he said that everything there was so green. I asked what he did there. All he could come up with at that moment was that he picked blueberries.

I didn't have much information to work with but I decided to try something Clementine Hunter had done and design a rug using the two-plane approach. I started in the lower right corner and drew the family apartment building. Beside it I drew a train leaving the Boston station and entering the tunnel Dad mentioned. In the upper plane, on the right, I drew the train emerging from the tunnel and arriving in Granville. A house like I imagine Aunt Alma and Uncle Bill might have had, with a friendly, breezy front porch, is portrayed on the left. My grandmother, my aunt, and my dad are in the middle of the rug picking blueberries. A narrow border with squares in the

corners was all that was needed.

As I've described these memory rugs to you I've also described my design processes to encourage you to begin putting what you know on paper. Your attention will become focused on the subject, one thought will lead to another, and soon you will be enthusiastically coming up with ideas to complete the picture. Sometimes you can fill in the blanks in the memories by reviewing old photos, visiting places, incorporating your own recollections, or, when all else fails, making something up. The accuracy of the details are not as important as preserving the essence of the past.

Soon it dawned on me that what my dad was seeing was not as exciting as what he was thinking.

Granville Summers
31" x 27 3/4"
Double-thickness, hand-cut wool strips hooked through primitive linen.

PHOTOGRAPH BY CHRIS SMITH.

THE ONLY BRIGHT PARTS IN *GRANVILLE SUMMERS* ARE THE OATMEAL CLOUDS. The rug portrays a happy memory and a bit brighter blue Granville sky would have been preferable. I need to round out my collection of blue wools to include slightly brighter sky blues. In contrast, the Boston sky is a gray windowpane plaid.

The house was hooked with three oatmeals. The porch is brightest, the top of the house is the medium value, and the bottom of the house, shaded by the porch roof, is the darkest value. The mountains were hooked with patches of greens representing the tops of different trees. People are simple shapes colored to contrast with their backgrounds. I had to hook solid greens around the little boy's shorts to distinguish them from their background. The blueberry bush was hooked with a blue plaid to avoid having to hook individual berries.

designing your own heirlooms

By now I hope I have inspired you to design a rug and hook an heirloom that will be treasured by younger generations. Think how wonderful it would be to come upon several old rugs rolled up in an attic or antique shop. Imagine that as you unrolled them you saw that they depicted buildings, people dressed in period clothing, or intriguing scenes you don't quite understand. Imagine that they included lettering indicating the location depicted in the rug. Imagine that you found a label on the back written in the rug maker's hand describing the item or event depicted along with the date the rug was completed, where it was hooked, and the signature of its creator. These could be your rugs, your memories, and your history in the years to come, preserved for posterity.

WITH OUR BUSY LIVES, WE SOMETIMES FORGET that it is up to us to create tomorrow's heirlooms. The handmade treasures we search through antique shops for were created by people who were probably just as busy as we are. Handiwork signed by the craftsman is rare and much more valuable than comparable anonymous work. Knowing a bit about the circumstances under which it was created is invaluable. How many things that you produce this year will remain in 50 or 100 years? Even insignificant events in the lives of people a century ago are intriguing to many of us today.

To encourage you to get started on preserving your past through a primitive pictorial, let's design some rugs together. One of my most popular designs is the *Nathaniel Lord 1799 House*, the one with the big flag. That is probably because we Americans as a people are particularly patriotic. Naturally the best time to look for flags is

Fourth of July week. As you go about your business take notice of an unusual display of an American flag.

I found such a display when I spied a flag tacked horizontally to the front of the one-story connector between a two-story house and its two-story barn. The mailbox said the place was the River Road Farm.

From my car window I took several photographs of the farm's interesting details as well as a couple of comprehensive shots showing how everything fit together. I got the film developed, looked at the overview shots, and pasted two photos together to form a panoramic version of the three structures.

Get a pencil or marker and a piece of paper and let's work together on this design. I start most of mine on a sheet of 6 $1/2$" x 9" lined notebook paper. When I hold the notebook horizontally the page size encourages designs

that are 1 $1/2$ times as wide as they are tall, a good proportion for rugs. We'll start on the left side of the sheet and draw a square, which will be the front of the two-story house. Now let's draw a rectangle on top of the square (make it equal in length with the square) to represent the roof and a rectangular chimney on top of the roof. Draw a rectangular centered window on the second story, leaving enough room underneath for a rectangular door. Draw that door and add a rectangular window on either side of it and the upper window. Voila! We have a house.

As I said, there is a long single-story connector between the house and barn. Because this is our first project and because our subject is so much longer than it is tall, let's set as our objective a pattern twice as long as it is wide and plan on finished dimensions of about 20" x 40". The buildings will run from end to end across the middle of the paper. We can

River Road

include a couple of trees for softness.

Let's return to our notebook
and draw the barn on the right of
the page. Keep the bottom level
with the bottom of the house. The
barn is bigger than the house and
the sides are a little higher than
the sides of the house. Draw its
straight sides and add a peaked
roof that's a little higher than the
house chimney.

Now draw the base of the
connector and the top and bottom
roof lines. The top roof line starts
at the top of the barn wall and the
bottom line is about in the middle
of the second-story windows.
Starting at the house end of the
connector, draw two windows, a
door, and a window. Starting at the
barn end draw a window close to
the barn, a horizontal flag shape,
then another window. Do you
have enough space? Actually there
is another door and two windows
I had to eliminate because they
wouldn't fit. My connector is

It is up to us to create tomorrow's heirlooms.

already twice as long as the main
house is wide and I don't want it
any wider. Also, I don't want a
long skinny rug. If you can't fit
everything, eliminate something
other than the flag.

Finish the barn by putting a
door at the edge close to the connector, a large center door, a
smaller door to the right, and a
short window between the center
door and the door on the left.
Place a trim line horizontally
across the front of the barn
halfway between the connector's
top and bottom roof lines. Then
place a short window above the
line the width of the large center
barn door. Draw two windows
side by side in the center of the
roof peak.

How's it looking? Let's add a
little softness. There are lots of
trees on the property, but let's center a big one in the space we left
between the two connector windows to the left of the flag. When
I draw deciduous trees, I think of
a bunch of tulips in a tight, clear,
glass vase. The stem tops spread,
burdened by the blossoms, just as
the main branches of a tree spread.
The gathered lower portions of
the stems combine to form a
trunk shape. For a winter tree
draw five or six main branches
from tip to trunk then add sec-
ondary branches to the primary
ones. For a leafed tree, draw an
irregular perimeter, representing
the foliage, an equal distance from
the branches. If you want you may
draw a hole or two in the foliage
where there aren't any branches so
sky can peek through. Once
you've drawn the foliage perimeter, erase the branches you don't
want to have showing.

Let's include the large pine

Your drawing can be simple because the fabrics you hook with will add color, texture, and personality.

tree behind the end of the connector and the barn. A pine tree is a center stalk with separated arm-like branches on both sides of it. There is space between the branches for irregular clumps of upturned foliage on the ends. The pine tree should be a little taller than the barn and of course should be narrow at the top and wider toward the bottom.

My house is looking pretty good. How is yours coming? Let's add more softness by placing a cedar tree to the left of the house. It reaches to the bottom roof line. A driveway leads from the barn door to the road at the left of the house. To create softness, make the driveway curved and irregular. Add a little irregularity to the buildings' base line also.

After adding $1/2$" to the left side, my drawing measures 5" x 10" inches, perfect when enlarged for a 20" x 40" rug. A simple 1" border will increase it to 22" x 42". To add "River Road Farm" above the bottom border, increase the rug height by 2" and center lettering in a 2" space between the drawing and the bottom border.

WHAT HAVE WE LEARNED?

FIRST, look around at things you see every day for subject matter. You don't have to portray earthshaking events. Fifty years from now this decade's everyday life will be a curiosity, and in the meantime it offers the elements of a good design.

SECOND, start simply. Draw something you know, something you can photograph or look at again and again, for you will prob-ably need to review its details.

THIRD, begin with what is easiest in the design, then move on to more difficult parts. We started with the simple main house at one end of the page, then drew the more complicated barn at the other. There were lots of trees to choose from, but by the time we had drawn the buildings we knew to choose the ones that softened and did not obscure the buildings.

FOURTH, think of the things you are trying to draw as geomet-ric shapes—squares, rectangles, tri-angles, circles, ovals, and so on. The house was a square topped by a rectangular roof and chimney. The doors and windows were simple rectangles.

FIFTH and most important of all, don't worry. Have fun. If you want to use graph paper as I did for some of my early rugs, you can do so to count squares, make straight lines, center everything, and draw in correct proportion. However, casually drawn rugs can be just as attractive and maybe even a bit more charming. Give it a try. Your drawing can be simple because the fabrics you hook with will add color, texture, and person-ality. Follow your instincts. I think you'll be pleased with the result.

I DREW AND HOOKED FOUR RUGS WITH JUST HOUSES IN THEM before I hooked one with people and pets. When you are ready for a new challenge, you can design a rug like my *Dog Lady* rug.

I walk my three dogs twice daily. I know some of my hooking students have described me to their friends and relatives and everyone seems to know who I am now. I bumped into a man at a holiday party who gave me a warm "Hello" despite not being sure how he knew me. Finally he exclaimed, "Oh, you're the dog lady!" That conversation inspired my *Dog Lady* rug.

It's pretty easy for me to draw my own pets, and I've found other people usually have little trouble drawing theirs. That's probably because we are intimately familiar with how they look. When I walk our dogs, Kelsie, our German Shepherd mix, pulls me forward. Mocha, the chocolate Lab, pokes along behind, digging her feet in and leaning away from me when I try to hurry her. Andy, our cocker spaniel, trots a bit behind me. If you are having trouble drawing your pet, try the following.

Dog Lady

Dog Lady
35" x 22"
Double-thickness, hand-cut wool strips
hooked through primitive linen.

PHOTOGRAPH BY CHRIS SMITH.

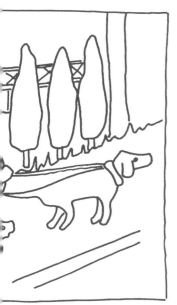

THE BUILDINGS IN MY *DOG LADY* RUG were hooked with four oatmeals. The woman's jacket was hooked in a small charcoal plaid that looks like a tweed when hooked. Her skirt is hooked with a soft cotton denim. The sidewalk is striped haphazardly with a variety of rust wools and its diagonal orientation pulls the viewer along it.

Note that two of the dogs' distant legs are hooked in less saturated colors, differentiating them and making them appear farther away. Their ears are defined with those same fabrics. The third dog is hooked with a tweed accurately representing its coloring. A tan plaid indicates the areas of lighter coloring on the dog's legs and stomach and is used to differentiate its ear.

I settled on a lavender sky after trying blue and tan, as the rug needed brightness. Blue blended with the greens and tan blended with the buildings, brown fence, and tree. Except for the sky, I didn't worry much about this rug, and I like the relaxed result. I had fun hooking this rug and I think it looks like I did.

dog
lady

Tory Chimneys

Reduce the animal to simple shapes. The body is an oval, the head is a circle (with an oval muzzle for dogs), and the tail and legs are sausage shapes. Their back legs have hips, but you don't have to get that technical. My dogs are drawn simply, yet if you met them you would recognize them. Note that Kelsie and Mocha are smooth and Andy's bumpy outline indicates that his fur is curly.

If you have trouble drawing animals, you can trace a photo or drawing and enlarge it. I recommend clear plastic (sheet protector weight) to trace on and a Sharpie Ultra Fine Point permanent marker. Outline the animal's body, tail, legs, and ears. Add eyes and a nose. Don't be tempted to include details. Simple, generalized shapes are most effective in primitive rugs. Enlarge or reduce the tracing to fit in your design.

I don't recommend tracing house photos, however. Houses in standard-size photos are tiny and it is tempting to include a lot of detail. Unless the photo was taken with a wide-angle lens, it is hard to get a truly frontal view, the easiest view to hook. Individual trees in a stand of trees cannot usually be identified, and hooking the intermeshed foliage of a group of trees is hard to do effectively. I indicate a group of trees with several clearly separate trees. The only time I draw a mass of foliage is in a distant background, and then I include one or two small, clearly defined trees to eliminate any viewer uncertainty.

BEFORE WE GO ON TO ANOTHER DESIGN LESSON, let's review what we've learned already. Our first project, *River Road Farm*, was a simple structure that could be photographed or revisited when more information was needed. Many of the problems people encounter when drawing are caused by not really knowing what an object looks like. In order to draw something, one has to be able to recon-

Begin with what is easiest in the design, then move on to more difficult parts.

Halloween

struct it, not merely recognize it. When I start to sketch something, I often discover that I don't know exactly what it looks like (my Halloween rug, which I'll discuss in a minute, is a good example). If you can't visit the subject of your rug, then consult photos, books, magazines, and even greeting cards to obtain more information. Collect pictures as references to study shapes and colors.

OUR SECOND PROJECT, *Dog Lady*, contained inanimate as well as animate objects. People and animals are harder to draw because they move and change. Unless we photograph them, we have to draw them the way they probably looked. Our strategy in this rug was to reduce each object to its simplest form, ignoring the details.

OUR THIRD PROJECT, *Tory Chimneys*, contains inanimate and animate objects and symbolism. We use symbolism to tell a story with-

Hooking a primitive rug is a beautiful way of preserving the past.

out words. In order to get our point across, the symbols have to be clear.

Tory Chimneys, a house down my street, is supposedly haunted. The house is a wonderful two-and-a-half story building with two or three smaller buildings attached to its side and back. The house is painted light brown with brick-red window mullions and blue doors. The chimneys are white with black bands at the top.

As I remember the story, the ghost is a woman carrying a candle who appears on the house's stairway. She is believed to be a

former resident of the house whose children were abducted by Indians. At the time, Indians kidnapped women and children and took them to Canada, where they sold them as slaves. I believe the kidnapping took place along the river near Durrell's bridge.

Working in two planes enabled me to combine all of these elements in a rectangular rug. The house is on the lower plane and the story of its ghostly inhabitant is in the upper.

I turned to my notebook and casually drew the house and its attachments in the middle of the lower horizontal plane. There is a modern Florida room at the far right that I omitted, but I did include a portion of the house's unusual fence.

Next I drew a stair profile and a female figure standing on it. To her right is the winding path of the Kennebunk River as I

**I hope that, through my words and rugs,
I have inspired you
to create a work of hand and heart
that will be treasured
by a textile lover yet to be born.**

observed it from Durrell's bridge. To her left are two Indians, each carrying a child into the woods. To fill the empty spaces in the bottom plane I drew the huge maple tree that grows on the lawn in front of the house and an imaginary tree at the end of the fence.

This complex rug employs the same techniques as the simple rugs described at the beginning of this chapter. With the exception of the river, the only thing that is more complicated is the idea. To portray an involved situation in a primitive rug, think symbolically. A woman standing on stairs above a house suggests a supernatural event. People with feather headdresses and fringed clothing must be Indians, and the children are pushing against them trying to break free. The body of water is obviously a river spanned by a simple bridge.

FOR OUR FOURTH PROJECT we will design a rug based entirely on a secondhand account, having never seen any of the elements of the design. Two of my sisters told me a story my dad had told them about how one Halloween his junior choir rehearsed in the church belfry. That was a great image for a rug, except I didn't know how to depict it.

Sadly, my dad has passed away, and no one is sure which church he attended at the time of his experience, so there is no way of knowing what his church looked like. I

leafed through my primitive painting books looking for stone churches like those often seen in cities. The one I found had its bell tower as a separate structure, unlike the rooftop bell towers I was used to seeing here in Maine. Seeing that kind of tower enabled me to visualize how to fit an entire choir and bells in one rectangular space.

I portrayed the choir director as a tall man in a black robe facing a group of people half his height wearing red robes. I drew this easy part first in the lower half of my notebook page. (I doubt Dad's choir wore robes for practice, but the robes symbolize the group's function.) The difference in the robe colors accentuates the difference in height between the director and the children.

From looking at church pictures I confirmed that there must have been openings in the belfry to allow the sound of the bells to escape. I opted for hanging bells so the choir could stand underneath them. Now I needed to make this scene look like Halloween. Bats flying through the sky outside the tower openings would be good, as would a huge harvest moon and jack-o'-lanterns. The rug could be hooked with an orange glow on the interior objects. How about a black cat wandering by with his back arched?

I could have done a better job had I talked to my dad about the memory, but that opportunity

was lost. I could have also done nothing, and this story would have been forgotten. It's amazing what you can create when you start with what you know, do a little research, concentrate on important concepts, ignore unimportant details, and use your imagination.

I HOPE THAT, THROUGH MY WORDS AND RUGS, I have inspired you to create a work of hand and heart that will be treasured by a textile lover yet to be born. I've suggested a variety of design sources, from sketching your own house to recording a dear one's recollections. Thanks to my dad's memory rugs I have my mom reminiscing about her own childhood. Together we are designing a series of rugs depicting Noden family activities from the 1920s. That collaboration alone reinforces my belief that hooking a primitive rug is a beautiful way of preserving the past.

BOTH OLD AND NEW WOOLENS find their way into my rugs. When I'm in a fabric store I always check the remnant section for unusual woolens. I'm a big fan of mail order, too. The advertisers in *Rug Hooking* magazine will send you sample swatches of what they sell. Buy 1-yard pieces of neutral background if you like mixed backgrounds; otherwise purchase 1 1/2-yard or 2-yard pieces, which is enough for most medium-sized rugs. Accumulate a variety of 1/2-yard pieces of colorful tweeds, checks, and plaids.

The best hooking wool is 100 percent wool flannel (skirt weight). Some blends are also acceptable (80/20 or 70/30 wool/nylon). Disassemble all used clothing, removing all zippers, buttons, and so forth. Clean both new and used material prior to cutting it. Wash it in warm water with a small amount of liquid laundry detergent and rinse it in cold water. Dry it in your dryer's normal cycle to fluff it.

All of my rugs are hooked on a foundation of Angus burlap, premium primitive burlap, or premium primitive linen. I bind all of my rugs with rug tape, usually black or brown to match the outer row of hooking. Pin your tape on your foundation before you sew, as the foundation can stretch. Sew the tape on (by hand or by machine) before you begin to hook. If you wait until you have hooked the edge you will have a hard time get-

ting the tape close enough to your hooking to cover the foundation. Then put in a zigzag or double straight stitch 3/4" outside the tape to prevent the foundation from unraveling.

I always tear or cut my strips by hand, from 1/4" to 3/8" for single thickness and 3/8" to 1/2" for double. I cut with Fiskars Softouch shears. To make my rugs look more primitive and less uniform I stopped cutting with a machine and began using scissors. However, it wasn't long before I found myself cutting neatly between threads on each piece of fabric, almost as neatly as if I were still using the machine. My house gets messy at times, but my handiwork is always neat whether I want it to be or not.

AS TO THE OTHER EQUIPMENT I USE, I prefer a primitive hook, and I cut tails with embroidery scissors. I hook on a Puritan frame but recommend a 14" round quilting hoop to beginners as an economical alternative. A frame stand is useful for 2' x 3' and larger rugs. Without a stand the weight of a big rug pulls the frame forward out of your lap.

Place your completed rug, hooking side down, on several layers of terry cloth towels and put a damp pressing cloth on top of it. Steam press the rug, pressing lightly to let the steam shrink any bulges. Repeatedly lift and press the iron until the rug is flat. Press the foundation's corners diagonally

close to the tape, then turn the rug face up and press the foundation's edges under about two threads beyond the binding.

After pressing the rug I trim the foundation just outside the binding tape. I turn back the tape and slipstitch the hem using upholstery thread, an embroidery needle, and a leather thimble.

Attach a label to the back of your rug containing handwritten information about the rug. Include such things as your name, the date, where the rug was hooked, and a bit of information about the rug's materials or its subject matter. To make the label, cut out a triangular paper pattern and pin its long edge even with the selvage of a piece of thin wool gabardine—choose a fabric color light enough to show writing, yet dark enough to hide dirt. Cut out the fabric label and write on it with a brown or olive-green fabric pen. Tuck the raw label edges between the rug and the binding tape, then sew it on.

For a catalog of my patterns please write to me at Port Primitives, PO Box 2798, Kennebunkport, ME 04046 or contact any of the fine businesses listed below:

A Primitive Pastime
N4 W22496 Bluemound Road
Waukesha, WI 53186
(262) 513–9005

Cabin Creek
8252 Military Road
Woodbury, MN 55129
(651) 459-9684

Crow Hill Primitives
4 Westvale Road
Kennebunkport, ME 04046

DiFranza Designs
25 Bow Street
North Reading, MA 01864-2553
(978) 664-2034

The Dorr Mill Store
PO Box 88
Guild, NH 03754
(800) 846-DORR.

Hoss-Town Cottage Classics
P.O. Box 449
Cherry Valley, IL 61016
(815) 397-0644

Kindred Spirits
115 Colonial Lane
Kettering, OH 45429
(937) 435-7758

L.J. Fibers
4750 Grand Avenue South
Minneapolis, MN 55409
(612) 827–2397

Northwoods Wool
P.O. Box 1027
Cumberland, WI 54829
(715) 822–3198

Patsy B
P.O. Box 1050
South Orleans, MA 02662
(508) 240-0346

Pine Island Primitives
861 Balsam Court NE
Pine Island, MN 55963
(507) 356–2908

Primitive Pastimes
410 Walnut Hill Road
North Yarmouth, ME 04097
(207) 829–3725

Primitive Spirit
445 W. 19th Avenue
Eugene, OR 97401
(541) 344-4316

Primitive Wool Creek
3713 Flowermeadow Street
Joliet, IL 60431
(815) 725–6802

Primitive Woolens
P. O. Box 251282
Plano, TX 75025–1282
Pat Brooks (615) 230–5925
Jeanne Smith (972) 542–4404

Quail Hill Designs
258 Pennellville Road
Brunswick, ME 04011-7926
(207) 729–0299

The Red Saltbox
204 S. Third Street
Miamisburg, OH 45342
(973) 847–2162

Turkey Hollow Primitives
(203) 263–0426

W. Cushing & Company
PO Box 351
Kennebunkport, ME 04046
(800) 626-7847.

Wood N Wool
6400 Canon Wren
Austin, TX 78746
(512) 431–0431

Woolen Memories
20 Glendale Circle
Ware, MA 01082
(413) 967–4970

Woolley Fox LLC
123 Woolley Fox Lane
Ligonier, PA 15658
(724) 238–3004